BED AND BREAKFAST

Alaska Style!

EDITED BY
Cass Crandall

ILLUSTRATIONS BY
Diana Tillion

Kachemak Publishing
Homer, Alaska

<u>On the cover:</u>
FRONT — The Log House Bed & Breakfast, Eagle River (p.90)
BACK (top to bottom) — Captain Bligh's Beaver Creek Lodge
and Guide Service, Soldotna (p. 133); Peters Creek Inn,
Chugiak (p. 92); 7 Gables Inn, Fairbanks (p. 190).

COPYRIGHT © 1995 by Cass Crandall

PRINTED AND BOUND IN THE UNITED STATES OF AMERICA

ISBN 0-9626071-5-0

ISSN 1053-4989

Library of Congress Catalog Card Number: 94-073723

PUBLISHED BY
Kachemak Publishing
P.O. Box 470
Homer, AK 99603

DESIGNED BY
Kathy Doogan

EDITORIAL ASSISTANCE
L.J. Campbell

CONTENTS

BED AND BREAKFAST
Alaska Style!

Introduction

Welcome to the 4th Edition of *Bed and Breakfast Alaska Style!* It is hard to believe five years have passed since our first edition came out. It's true...time *does* fly when you're having fun! Many B&Bs have come and gone in those five years. For some, the business just hasn't worked out. But there are also many B&B hosts for whom the extra income and the heartfelt praise and appreciation of their guests have been sufficiently rewarding to keep them going, rising early with a cup of coffee and a smile to greet each new traveler who comes their way. As we welcome those new B&Bs just starting out, we must also extend warm congratulations to those who have stuck with it.

One notable change over the years seems to be that many visitors are coming back. It used to be that Alaska was viewed by the rest of our countrymates as foreign soil: a difficult place to get to (by dog sled), with chilly accommodations (igloos), unusual food (muktuk) and possibly unfriendly hosts (bearded roughnecks wearing plaid). However, that has all changed. Now, visitors find that Alaska isn't really any harder to get to than

Cleveland, our homes are warm and cozy, the food is the same as anywhere else and, thanks to Eddie Bauer and L.L. Bean, now *everyone* wears plaid. As a result, it is becoming more common to hear that someone is enjoying a third or fourth visit instead of their first. They must be having fun!

In this 4th Edition of *Bed and Breakfast Alaska Style!* we list more than 100 of the nicest spots you'd care to visit, with attentive hosts, comfortable beds and good food. Please take your time when browsing through this book, and be sure to try the delicious recipes. I especially like the looks of "John Wayne's Favorite Recipe" (page 71), prepared by the hosts at the Little Rabbit Creek B&B. We are also looking forward to trying the cranberry scones on page 82, a speciality of the Valley of the Moon B&B.

So, take the time to come and visit — we know you'll love it here!

—*Cass Crandall*
Homer, Alaska

ABOUT THIS BOOK

The following credit card abbreviations have been used throughout the book:

AMEX — American Express   **CB** — Carte Blanche
DC — Diner's Club   **DS** — Discover
MC — Mastercard   **VISA** — not abbreviated

Some Alaska communities charge bed taxes or other local taxes on accommodations. Unless otherwise indicated, the prices given in this book do not include those local taxes.

Prices given were current as of January 1995. Since prices are always subject to change, be sure to check these details with the B&B hosts before making plans.

RESERVATION
SERVICES

ACCOMMODATIONS ON THE KENAI

P.O. Box 2956
Soldotna, Alaska 99669
(907) 262-2139
Coordinator: Suzanne Richards

Hours: 24, year-round
Credit Cards: MC, VISA (to hold telephone
reservations until deposit is received by personal check)

Accommodations on the Kenai is a referral service for lodgings in Soldotna, Kenai, Sterling, Kasilof and Ninilchik. Suzanne has personally visited and inspected each bed and breakfast in AOK's directory to assure guests of quality, courteous and safe lodgings during their stays on the beautiful Kenai Peninsula. She can also book king salmon and halibut fishing charters and other tours.

Your best interests are in mind when Suzanne books your accommodations. A year-round resident of the Kenai Peninsula, she has several years experience in the hospitality field.

DEPOSIT AND REFUND POLICY: A deposit of 50 percent is required to confirm reservations.

ALASKA PRIVATE LODGINGS STAY WITH A FRIEND

P.O. Box 200047
Anchorage, Alaska 99520-0047
(907) 258-1717; Fax (907) 258-6613
Coordinator: Mercy Dennis

Hours: 9 am to 6 pm in summer;
variable winter hours
Credit Cards: AMEX, MC, VISA
Range of Rates:
Moderate $45-$60
Average $61-$70
Luxury $71 and up
Number of Host Homes: Approximately 100

Alaska Private Lodgings offers bed and breakfast homes throughout Southcentral and Southeast Alaska, with the largest number of listings available in Anchorage. Coordinator Mercy Dennis sends out a free brochure and for $5 will also send a descriptive directory with a complete listing of her host homes, with information about rates, breakfasts, types of bed and breakfast accommodations available (rooms, suites and cabins), and choice of settings.

Alaska Private Lodgings promises you'll find comfortable, clean accommodations and "an easy and convenient Alaska with local directions, dining suggestions and sightseeing recommendations provided by friendly Alaskan hosts."

"Bed and Breakfast travelers are treated more like welcome guests than paying customers. A B&B is not just a place to stay, but an opportunity to meet local residents, enjoy people with common interests, and learn about sights and specialties known only by Alaskan 'sourdoughs.'"

DEPOSIT AND REFUND POLICY: Deposits will be refunded with 96 hours cancellation notice. Cancellation 96 hours or less prior to arrival date or "no show" will forfeit one night's accommodation rate. Deposit will be fully refunded if we are unable to satisfy your reservation request.

HOMER REFERRAL AGENCY

P.O. Box 1264
Homer, AK 99603
(907) 235-8996 or (907) 235-8998
Fax (907) 235-2625
Coordinators: Floyd and Gert Seekins

Hours: 24, year-round
Credit Cards: MC, Visa
Range of Rates: $40-$125
Number of Host Homes: Approximately 50

Homer Referral Agency does it all with just one phone call — bookings for bed and breakfasts, activities, tours, fishing and boat trips — for Homer, Anchor Point, Seldovia, Port Graham and Halibut Cove. This agency connects clients with virtually any accommodations — in town, out-of-town, honeymoon cabins or suites, lodgings for travelers with children or pets, smokers, non-smokers, with kitchen facilities, hot tubs, saunas, fantastic views — all with no charge to the client.

The staff at Homer Referral Agency has personally inspected all of the recommended properties. The agency's goal is for clients to have the best Alaska vacations possible at homes away from home, and toward that goal, to match clients with hosts and hostesses of similar interests.

Homer Referral Agency also books completely furnished apartments, homes and guest cabins nightly or weekly without breakfast.

DEPOSIT AND REFUND POLICY: Either the first night's lodging and 50 percent of the remainder must be paid in full or a credit card number must be given to confirm reservations. Homer Referral Agency's homes accept personal checks, traveler's checks or cash. On receipt of deposit, Homer Referral Agency will send you a receipt and a map to the host home. No charge is made for cancellations if the rooms can be rebooked.

BED AND BREAKFAST HOMES

SOUTHEAST ALASKA

Called the Alaska Panhandle, Southeast is where the beauty of the state begins. Because of its southerly location, the weather here is warmer than in the rest of the state, with temperatures rarely falling below zero in winter. The terrain is predominately mountainous, with most communities stretched along the shore of the mainland or located on islands. Glaciers abound here and many are located close enough to the towns to be easily viewed or visited. The sparkling waters of Southeast are teeming with marine life such as whales, sea lions, seals and many kinds of fish.

GUSTAVUS

Known as the gateway to Glacier Bay National Park, Gustavus is 48 miles northwest of Juneau, accessible by boat or air. Unique in an otherwise mountainous terrain, Gustavus was homesteaded as an agricultural community because of its miles of level land. Residents today support themselves by fishing or working in tourism or for the National Park Service. In addition to the park, the area is popular because of its sport fishing, berrypicking, birdwatching, beachcombing and kayaking.

For more information contact:

Gustavus Visitors Association
P.O. Box 167
Gustavus, Alaska 99826

A PUFFIN'S BED AND BREAKFAST LODGE

P.O. Box 3
Gustavus, Alaska 99826
(907) 697-2260; in Alaska (800) 478-2258
Fax (907) 697-2258
Sandy and Chuck Schroth, Hosts

Months Open: May 1 to September 15
Hours: 24
Credit Cards: None
Accommodations: 5 cabins and Puffin Lodge
Children Welcome: Yes
Pets Accommodated: Yes
Social Drinking: Yes
Smoking: Outside

ROOM RATES*
Single w/private bath: $40 - $75
Double w/private bath: $70 - $75
Each additional person: $20
Children 2 to 12: $10 (under 2 free)
(*All are guest cabins which sleep 3 to 6 people.)

A Puffin's Bed and Breakfast is within walking distance of restaurants, grocery stores, the community park and river fishing spots in central Gustavus. The Schroths will meet you on arrival and give you a tour of the town on the way to their four-acre homestead.

Puffin's offers five modern cabins with comfortable beds, all attractively decorated with Alaska art prints and crafts. The cabins — named Salmon, Halibut, Orca, Sea Otter and Whale — can comfortably accommodate from three to six people. Three cabins have sparkling clean private baths, located in a separate building just down a flower-bordered path, while the other two have attached baths. A new outdoor barbecue and picnic area is also available for guest use. One cabin and Puffin Lodge are wheelchair accessible, and the lodge has a dining and social area, handicap-access bath, library full of Alaskana books and private conference room.

The Schroths also operate Puffin Travel, a year-round, full travel service, and can set you up with reservations for sight-seeing, fishing, tour boats, accommodations and travel.

For breakfast—served at Puffin Lodge anytime before 9 a.m.—expect delicious waffles, pancakes, French toast or eggs and toast with local jams and syrups. The coffee pot is always on at the lodge and there is a hot pot and coffee, tea, and hot chocolate in each cabin.

"A Puffin's Bed and Breakfast offers free travel services in addition to our bed and breakfast, emphasizing a peaceful, successful, genuine Alaskan experience."

—Sandy and Chuck

PUFFIN'S FRENCH TOAST

2 eggs
2 C milk
1 t cinnamon
1/2 t nutmeg
Sourdough bread slices

Mix first four ingredients with whisk. Dip both sides of bread into egg mixture; fry in margarine until light brown on both sides. Microwave one minute, or until done.

Sift confectioners' sugar over French toast and serve with fresh fruit.

GLACIER BAY COUNTRY INN
BED AND BREAKFAST

P.O. Box 5
Gustavus, Alaska 99826
(907) 697-2288
Al and Annie Unrein, Innkeepers

Months Open: May to September
Hours: 24
Credit Cards: None
Accommodations: 9 rooms
Children Welcome: All ages
Pets Accommodated: No
Social Drinking: Yes
Smoking: No

ROOM RATES*
Single: w/shared bath, $119; w/private bath, $149
Double w/private bath: $238
Each additional adult: $69
Children: $54
(*Rates are based on the American Plan, which
includes breakfast, lunch and dinner.)

Glacier Bay Country Inn is located four miles from the Gustavus Airport, and about six miles from Glacier Bay National Park headquarters at Bartlett Cove. The Inn sits at the center of the Unreins' 160-acre homestead, where they cut hay and logs and run a sawmill when they are not gardening or picking berries and mushrooms.

The Inn's log beam ceilings, dormer windows, multigabled roof and large porches create the comfortable, relaxed atmosphere of a true country inn. In the rooms, guests find warm flannel sheets, cozy comforters and fluffy towels.

The Unreins offer several tour packages, combining accommodations at the Inn with various boat tours of Glacier Bay, salmon and halibut fishing charters, and whale-watching trips. Bicycles are available for touring Gustavus, and there are miles of beaches on which to beachcomb and daydream.

Glacier Bay Country Inn offers fabulous gourmet meals.

For breakfast, guests might enjoy such treats as crepes with whipped cream, apple dumplings or blueberry streusel muffins. For dinner, there might be halibut bisque, Dungeness crab with melted butter, and rhubarb custard pie. The Unreins also serve afternoon tea accompanied by hazelnut shortbread or coconut chews.

"The minute our guests arrive they can start to relax and enjoy their vacation. We'll meet them at the airport and take over from there! They won't have to worry about where to go for dinner, or how to get to the boat tours. Our expert chef is an artist with foods; everything looks as good as it tastes. Meals feature local seafoods, garden produce and homemade breads and desserts, but special diets can be accommodated with advance notice."

—Al and Annie

GOOD RIVERBED AND BREAKFAST

Box 37
Gustavus, Alaska 99826
Phone And Fax: (907) 697-2241
Sandy Burd, Hostess

Months Open: Memorial Day to Labor Day
Hours: 24
Credit Cards: None
Accommodations: 4 rooms, 1 cabin
Children Welcome: Yes
Pets Accommodated: No
Social Drinking: Yes
Smoking: Outside

ROOM RATES
Single: $50
Double: $50-$75
Guest cabin (sleeps two): $50

Good Riverbed and Breakfast is on the banks of the Good River in Gustavus at the mouth of Glacier Bay. Large picture windows overlook the garden and river, which flows to Icy Strait. Behind the house is a waterfowl refuge where geese and cranes stop by the thousands during their annual migrations.

The bed and breakfast is a spacious three-story log house made of Sitka spruce with classic dovetail corners, maple hardwood floors, exposed wooden beams, handmade tiles and many hand-crafted touches that will delight guests' aesthetic senses. Many original paintings by Alaska artists grace the walls and handmade patchwork quilts cover every bed. Guests can relax and browse through the library, write letters in the comfortable sitting room, tour the garden or root cellar, play the harpsichord, indulge in a game of badminton, or explore the area on one of the bikes provided for guests to use.

Breakfast at Good Riverbed includes homemade breads, freshly baked muffins and cakes, berry jams made on the premises, locally smoked salmon, fruit, juice, and special treats like blueberry flapjacks with spruce tip syrup or apple crepes with nagoonberry sauce. Everything is made from scratch using natural ingredients.

Make Good Riverbed your home base for a visit to Glacier Bay. The hosts can help you plan and make reservations for tour boats, kayaks, charter fishing and flights over the bay.

GOOSEBERRY MUFFINS

2 C flour (1 1/2 C white flour and 1/2 C mixed whole grain
      flours—I use whole wheat, oat, barley and graham)
2 t baking powder
1/2 C nuts (walnut, hazelnuts, or sunflower seeds are good)
1 egg beaten into 1 C milk
1/4 C spruce tip syrup (see note)
1/4 C melted butter
1 C fresh gooseberries (or currants or blueberries)

Preheat oven to 400 degrees. Mix all wet ingredients in one bowl and dry in another. Add wets to dry, add berries and fold together lightly until just mixed. (Do not overmix or muffins will be tough.) Bake for 20 minutes. Serve immediately with butter.

(Note: Spruce tip syrup is a regional specialty made each spring from the new spruce growth. Tips are picked, boiled in water to a sypury consistency, then strained and sweetened. Substitute maple or any type of fruit syrup in the recipe.)

HAINES

Haines is the site of the first and only U.S. Army post in Alaska until World War II; it was deactivated in 1946 and sold to private investors. Plans for development fell through, but the barracks and houses still stand as private homes, and the site has a parade ground, hotel and several tourist attractions. Today the post is a national historic site known as Fort William H. Seward. Attractions in and around Haines include:

◊ Walking Tour of Fort William H. Seward: Takes you past the historic buildings of the Army post, including the commanding officers' quarters, the guard house, the gymnasium and movie house, the barracks and the former cable office.

◊ Sheldon Museum and Cultural Center: Open daily from 1 p.m. to 5 p.m. during summer, the Museum is known for its collection of Tlingit and Russian artifacts.

◊ Eagles: The world's greatest concentration of eagles can be found at the Chilkat Bald Eagle Preserve near Haines from October through January. Some 3,500 eagles gather on the Chilkat River flats and in nearby trees to feed on the river's late run of salmon.

◊ Hiking Trails: There are several good hiking trails in the Haines area, ranging from the 2.4-mile B-Henry Point trail to the strenuous Mount Ripinski trail.

◊ Southeast Alaska State Fair: Held in August, the fair includes arts and crafts, food booths, garden produce competitions and a horse show.

For more information contact:

Haines Chamber of Commerce
P.O. Box 518
Haines, Alaska 99827
(907) 766-2202

THE SUMMER INN
BED AND BREAKFAST

117 Second Avenue North
P.O. Box 1198
Haines, Alaska 99827
(907) 766-2970
Mary Ellen and Bob Summer, Hosts

Months Open: Year-round
Hours: 24
Credit Cards: MC, VISA
Accommodations: 5 rooms
Children Welcome: Yes
Pets Accommodated: No
Social Drinking: No
Smoking: No

ROOM RATES
Single: $60 (summer) $50 (winter)
Double: $70 (summer) $60 (winter)
Triple: $90 (summer) $80 (winter)
Children: $10
Each additional person: $15

The Summer Inn is a five-bedroom historical house built by Tim Vogel, a member of Skagway's notorious Soapy Smith gang of the Klondike gold rush era.

The guest rooms are warm and inviting. Enjoy the Alaska art and books or write a letter at the large oak dining table. Coffee, tea and muffins are offered in the evening after your soak in the antique bathtub. Sourdough pancakes and ham or eggs and sausage are served with fruit, juice, coffee and tea to start your day before taking off to sightsee or photograph the eagles at the Chilkat Bald Eagle Preserve.

"The Summer Inn Bed and Breakfast is one of the oldest homes in Haines, tastefully renovated to preserve the historical significance of the time period. We invite you to make the Summer Inn your home while in Haines."

—Mary Ellen and Bob

JUNEAU-DOUGLAS

Juneau, Alaska's capital, was founded in the 1880s when Joe Juneau and Dick Harris discovered gold in a nearby creek. Douglas is a short drive away, directly across Gastineau Channel. The two towns, with a combined population of around 28,000, make up one of the most scenic "cities" in America. As state capital, major commercial fishing port and tourism center, Juneau is usually bustling with activity, while Douglas is much slower-paced. Juneau offers a variety of attractions, including:

◊ Capitol Building: Built in 1931, the Capitol houses the legislature and governor's office. With its extensive marble-work and painted murals, it's worth a visit.

◊ Governor's Mansion: While not open to the public, the Governor's Mansion is worth a peek from the outside, whether you are walking or driving on Calhoun Avenue.

◊ Alaska State Museum: A complete display of Alaska's history, from the Russian fur trade era to the trans-Alaska pipeline, as well as Alaska Native artifacts and an eagle's nest.

◊ Mines and mining: There are many gold mines in the Juneau/Douglas area including the Alaska-Juneau Mine on the Juneau side of the channel and the Treadwell Mine in Douglas.

◊ Mendenhall Glacier: This glacier can be reached by paved road and has a visitors center with an audio-visual room.

◊ Eaglecrest Ski Area: On Douglas Island, Eaglecrest is popular in summer and winter and offers tremendous views.

For more information, contact:

Juneau Convention & Visitors Bureau
134 third Street
Juneau, Alaska 99801
(907) 586-2201

BLUEBERRY LODGE
BED AND BREAKFAST

9436 North Douglas Highway
Juneau, Alaska 99801
Phone and Fax: (907) 463-5886
Jay and Judy Urquhart, Hosts

Months Open: Year-round
Hours: 24
Credit Cards: None
Accommodations: 5 rooms
Children Welcome: Yes
Pets Accommodated: Possibly
Social Drinking: Yes
Smoking: In covered exterior area

ROOM RATES
Single: $75 (summer) $65 (winter)
Double: $85 (summer) $75 (winter)
Each additional person: $10
Children: Under 4 free
10% fee to travel agents

Blueberry Lodge Bed and Breakfast offers a rustic and cozy Alaska setting, yet is only minutes away from Juneau.

Located on more than an acre of woods, Blueberry Lodge overlooks Gastineau Channel, an inland waterway. Each massive log in the 4,000-square-foot home has been handcrafted by a Yukon logsmith. The panorama includes majestic mountains, the channel and Mendenhall Wetlands State Game Refuge. The combination of freshwater streams and tidelands creates a rich series of estuaries and meadows. An active eagle nest can be viewed from the lodge. Specialties of the house include ginger-bread pancakes with lemon curd, sourdough Belgian waffles with spruce-tip syrup, and homemade blueberry sausage.

Blueberry Lodge has been inspected and approved by AAA and is listed in their tour book. The lodge was called "architecturally spectacular" by Powder Ski Magazine. The entire lodge can be rented for special occasions such as retreats, weddings and family gatherings.

CRONDAHL'S BED AND BREAKFAST

626 5th Street
Juneau, Alaska 99801
(907) 586-1464
Judy and Jay Crondahl, Hosts

Months Open: Year-round
Hours: 24
Credit Cards: None
Accommodations: 2 rooms
Children Welcome: All ages
Pets Accommodated: Yes
Social Drinking: Yes
Smoking: No

ROOM RATES
Single: $55   Double: $65
Each additional person: $10

Located in downtown Juneau's historic Starr Hill neighbor-hood, Crondahl's Bed and Breakfast is just six blocks from the capitol and three blocks from the Mount Roberts trail. The home is adjacent to Chickenyard Park, Juneau's oldest public park.

There are two guest rooms available at Crondahl's. One has a double bed and views of downtown and the harbor, while the other has a double and twin bed. The main floor of the home includes a large, open kitchen, and dining and living room.

The hosts describe their bed and breakfast in verse:

Close to the woods
In the middle of town
Is a house where the breakfasts
Have earned great renown.
There are quiches, burritos,
And pancakes with fruit,
Coffee ground fresh,
And a good morning toot
On a brass horn so mellow
You'll stand up and cheer,
"What a great bed and breakfast!
I'm so glad I'm here!"

CRONDAHL'S BED AND BREAKFAST EGG BURRITOS

2 eggs per person
Tabasco sauce
cottage cheese
fresh parsley
mild salsa
sharp Cheddar cheese

Break eggs into bowl, add a couple of dashes of Tabasco sauce and beat thoroughly.

To make egg wrappers for burritos: Heat a very small (6" diameter) skillet and lightly brush with oil. Put approximately 1 tablespoon of egg in skillet (just enough to cover the bottom when skillet is tipped). Cook until brown on bottom. Turn and cook other side. Turn out onto waxed paper. Make two wrappers for each person.

Make filling: Loosely scramble remaining eggs. Mix with cottage cheese (about 1 cup for six people) and fresh parsley (about 2 tablespoons for same amount). Cover bottom of baking dish with salsa. (There is no need to grease the baking dish). Divide filling between egg wrappers. Roll each wrapper like a burrito and put in baking dish on top of salsa. Cover lightly with grated Cheddar cheese. At this point, the burritos may be refrigerated overnight. Preheat oven to 400 degrees. Bake about 10 to 15 minutes until cheese is melted and salsa bubbles.

EAGLE'S NEST BED AND BREAKFAST

P.O. Box 20537
Juneau, Alaska 99802
(907) 586-6378
Steve Irwin and Charlotte Carroll, Hosts

Months Open: Year-round
Hours: 8 am to 9 pm
Credit Cards: MC, VISA
Accommodations: 1 A-frame home with 2 rooms
Children Welcome: 12 and over
Pets Accommodated: No
Social Drinking: Yes
Smoking: Outside

ROOM RATES
Single: $70
Double: $85
Entire A-frame home (accommodates 6): $200

Eagle's Nest Bed and Breakfast, located on beautiful Douglas Island, is seven miles from downtown Juneau. Nearby are Fish Creek, where salmon and eagles abound, and Eaglecrest Ski Area. The Eagle's Nest area is perfect for hiking and exploring, with its breathtaking views of Lemon Creek and Mendenhall glaciers and frequent glimpses of eagles overhead. Other activities include fishing and sightseeing by boat, helicopter or plane.

Eagle's Nest has two guest bedrooms upstairs: the Wildflower Room and the Hummingbird Room, each with a queen-size bed. A queen-size sleeper sofa is available downstairs should five or six people traveling together wish to rent the entire A-frame. There is a private entrance, woodstove, barbecue, cable TV, VCR, washer and dryer, full kitchen, telephone and an outdoor hot tub.

A self-serve breakfast includes cereals, milk, coffee, tea, juice, muffins, toast, eggs and hash browns.

GOULD'S ALASKAN VIEW
BED AND BREAKFAST

P.O. Box 240861
Douglas, Alaska 99824-0861
(907) 463-1546
Carolyn and Alan Gould, Hosts

Months Open: May to December 15
Hours: Flexible
Credit Cards: None
Accommodations: One apartment
Children Welcome: 12 years and over
Pets Accommodated: No
Social Drinking: Yes
Smoking: No

ROOM RATES
Single: $75 (summer); less 10% in winter
Double: $85 (summer); less 10% in winter
Each additional person: $10
Children: $10

The hosts at Gould's Bed and Breakfast were born and raised in Juneau. Alan is a civil engineer with a private company and works his wire rope business on the side. Carolyn works for

the city of Juneau in its three libraries. She cross-country skis and hikes and knows the Juneau trail system well.

Gould's is located on Douglas Island, one mile (a pleasant 30-minute walk) from downtown Juneau. Public transportation is available two blocks away. Gould's has a beautiful view of Gastineau Channel, Mount Juneau, Mount Roberts and the city of Juneau. Binoculars are provided to watch the eagles and herons that sit in the trees outside or the occasional whale in the channel. Many local attractions and activities are nearby.

The guest area, a 700-square-foot apartment in the hosts' home, can accommodate up to three people. It has its own entrance, and includes one large bedroom with a queen and twin bed, a fully equipped kitchen, cable TV and private phone line. The unit has its own heat zone and water heater. Laundry facilities and an ironing station are available for a small charge.

Guests may choose continental or full breakfasts from a menu of six choices. Specialties include buttermilk blueberry pancakes, eggs à la goldenrod and a variety of homemade muffins. Coffee, tea, soft drinks and a small dish of candy are provided in the apartment.

Gould's Bed and Breakfast is perfect for privacy-loving travelers and honeymooners, where guests can find peace, quiet and seclusion — a place to rest after a busy day of sightseeing.

GOULD'S BRAN MUFFINS

2 C hot water
2 C All Bran cereal
4 C Bran Buds cereal
2 1/2 C sugar
1 C plus 2 T shortening or oil
4 eggs
1 qt. buttermilk
5 t soda
2 t salt
5 1/2 C flour

Pour hot water over All Bran and Bran Buds; let stand. Cream sugar, shortening and eggs; add buttermilk and blend well. Add bran. Sift together soda, salt and flour; add to bran mixture and blend well. Spoon into greased muffin tins; bake at 400 degrees for 16-20 minutes. Batter will keep 6 to 8 weeks in refrigerator.

THE LOST CHORD
BED AND BREAKFAST

2200 Fritz Cove Road
Juneau, Alaska 99801
(907) 789-7296
Jesse, Ellen and Christy Jones, Hosts

Months Open: Year-round
Hours: 6 am to 12 am
Credit Cards: None
Accommodations: 4 rooms
Children Welcome: Yes
Pets Accommodated: By arrangement
Social Drinking: Yes
Smoking: Outside on decks only

ROOM RATES*
Single: $50 (summer) $40 (winter)
Double: $55 (summer) $45 (winter)
King: $65 (summer) $50 (winter)
Suite: $85
Each additional person: $10
*$10 additional for a one-night booking

Twelve-and-a-half miles from Juneau on beautiful and scenic Fritz Cove Road is the Lost Chord Bed and Breakfast. Named for a music business, the Lost Chord is on a private, secluded beach overlooking Auke Bay.

Jesse, Ellen and Christy Jones' beach home has four spacious, unique guest rooms such as the Squirrel's Nest, a cozy single room with trundle bed, semi-private bath and vanity room, and the Seals Cove Suite, which has its own woodstove, a beautiful view of the cove, private bath, partial kitchen with dining area and sitting room.

In addition to their warm hospitality, the Jones provide binoculars and a spotting scope to use, a private beach for fishing and round-the-clock coffee and tea. Your hosts also offer airport, ferry or bus pick up, although there is a $5 charge for after-midnight pick ups. For breakfast, expect a hearty, full meal with juice, fruit, cereal and entree.

"[The Lost Chord] represents what people hold dear in Southeast Alaska: a quiet pocket of beach, a skiff riding gently at anchor, a stand of spruce on a rocky point. Outside the big front windows framing mountains and soft green islands, gulls dive to the water with messy splashes...(inside) two rockers look through branches of hemlock to blue-green water...fall asleep to the cry of gulls, the toot of a ferry, or rhythmic laps of the incoming tide."

—Sarah Eppenbach,
Alaska Airlines magazine (8/89)

PEARSON'S POND LUXURY INN

4541 Sawa Circle
Juneau, Alaska 99801-8723
(907) 789-3772; Fax (907) 789-6722
Steve and Diane Pearson, Hosts

Months Open: Year-round
Hours: 24 (hosted check in from 3 pm to 10 pm)
Credit Cards: CB, DC, MC, VISA
Accommodations: 2 junior suites, 1 room
Children Welcome: 3 years and up
Pets Accommodated: No
Social Drinking: Yes
Smoking: No

ROOM RATES
Fireside Room:
$89 single, $99 double (summer)
$69 single, $79 double (winter)
Pond View Junior Suite:
$109 single, $119 double (summer)
$79 single, $89 double (winter)
Forest View Junior Suite:
$109 single, $119 double, $139 triple (summer)
$79 single, $89 double, $109 triple (winter)
Add $30 summer, $20 winter for adjoining private bath.
Each additional person: $20 (maximum 3 in room)
Children: $20

Guests at Pearson's Pond Luxury Inn enjoy a suite retreat with all the private comforts of home. Three-guest junior suites/ rooms, each with private entry and separated by guest kitchens and baths, make up the first floor of this three-story, custom home. It is tucked in the forest in a rural area just five minutes from Mendenhall Glacier, the airport, ferry terminal, shops, Glacier Bay departures and popular attractions.

Visitors soothe their cares in an outdoor spa amid lush gardens, wild berries and a glacial duck pond. They can feed the wild ducks, row the boat amidst lily pads, watch for bald eagles overhead, enjoy an aromatic cappuccino or herbal tea, ride bikes to the glacier or take a nature walk along the river

trail nearby. The serene environment appeals to adults.

The Pearsons recommend dining alfresco on the adjoining deck amid "the healing sounds of nature" with Mendenhall Glacier as a picturesque backdrop. The room rate includes a full self-serve breakfast or a full-serve continental breakfast. There are off-site health club privileges and ski packages offered nearby. On-site rowboat, barbecue, laundry, bikes, light fishing gear, freezer, fax machine and office equipment are also available.

The ensuite private sitting and dining area includes cable TV, audio and video tapes and players, private phone line, robes, slippers, hair dryers, dining table, recliner or couch, a great view and beds with wonderful quilts.

The Fireside Room, with a cozy electric fireplace, overlooks the pond from its deck and is great for shorter stays. The Pond View Junior Suite is larger, with lots of storage and a lovely pond view reflected in a bank of custom mirrors or from its deck. The large Forest View Junior Suite has a queen hide-a-bed for an extra guest. The oak roll-top desk and wainscoting make the Forest View popular with executive travelers. Its private deck overlooks the forest from which guests may pick berries for breakfast.

PEARSON'S POND HAM BREAD

2 C warm water
1 T sugar
2 pkgs. dry yeast
4 to 5 C flour
2 t salt
1 to 2 lbs ham, cooked
1 egg white, beaten with 1 T water

Warm a medium large mixing bowl. Add warm water and sugar; sprinkle with dry yeast. After yeast has softened, stir in salt. Beat in flour, 1 cup at a time. Add another 1/2 cup or more flour and knead by machine or hand firmly and thoroughly until dough is smooth and dimpled. Form into ball and place in clean, warm bowl. Cover with damp towel. Let rise until about doubled.

Take cooked turkey ham or regular ham and grind in meat grinder or chop very, very fine. Set aside. (Use more or less to suit your taste).

Punch dough down lightly and divide into 4 roughly equal parts. Let rest 10 minutes. Roll out each on a lightly floured surface to a 10" x 18" rectangle. Begin rolling from the left side, sealing (by pressing) the roll against the rectangle with each half roll. After the first full roll, sprinkle a few tablespoons of ground ham along the sealed edge, roll over and seal again. Repeat until the entire rectangle has been rolled. Seal the ends and the final edge well. Place seam side down on lightly greased baking sheet which has been sprinkled with cornmeal. Repeat with three other dough parts. Slash top diagonally in several locations; paint with egg white mixture. Let rise until doubled.

Bake at 365 degrees for 20 minutes. Paint with remaining egg white mixture. Bake another 15 to 20 minutes. Cool on racks.

SUTTON PLACE BED AND BREAKFAST

205 Seward Street
Juneau, Alaska 99801
(907) 463-3232
Max Sutton, Host

Months Open: May to October
Hours: 24
Credit Cards: None
Accommodations: One apartment
Children Welcome: All ages
Pets Accommodated: Yes
Social Drinking: Yes
Smoking: No

ROOM RATES
Single: $75
Double: $75
Each additional person: $10
Children: Under 10 free

Sutton Place Bed and Breakfast offers total privacy — a large downtown apartment with TV, VCR, phone and laundry facilities. This 650-square-foot studio apartment occupies the second story of a 1920's building, one block west of the Baranof Hotel, uphill from the Sportsman Barbershop.

This light, spacious, one-room apartment has a 10-foot-high ceiling, modern furnishings, two queen-size futons, and a private kitchen and bathroom.

A continental breakfast of fresh muffins, fruit, cereals, tea, coffee, and bread with jams, honey and butter is provided, plus popcorn for snacking. Max, your host, can be contacted if you have requests; otherwise guests enjoy the independence of having their own conveniently located, private studio.

Area activities and interests include hiking, cab and bus tours to Mendenhall Glacier, Mendenhall River rafting, kayaking, racquetball, tennis, gift shopping and fishing. Max runs the Sportsman Barbershop (at the bottom of the stairs to the B&B), and will "be happy to share the freshest rumors as to where and what the fish are biting."

PELICAN

Located on the northwest coast of Chichagof Island, Pelican can be reached by scheduled air service from Juneau or by the Alaska state ferry. Residents of this small village of 250 earn their living primarily from commercial fishing (the Fairweather salmon fishing grounds are nearby) and seafood processing. Like many Southeast communities, Pelican's homes and other buildings are connected by a system of boardwalks extending the length of town. Visitor activities include sightseeing, sport fishing for salmon and halibut, berry picking and hiking.

LISIANSKI INLET LODGE
BED AND BREAKFAST

P.O. Box 776
Pelican, Alaska 99832
(907) 735-2266
Gail Corbin, Hostess

Months Open: May 1to September 20
Hours: 24
Credit Cards: None
Accommodations: 3 rooms, 1 cabin
Children Welcome: Yes
Pets Accommodated: Yes
Social Drinking: Yes
Smoking: Outside

ROOM RATES*
Single: $110-$160
Double: $110-$130
Guest Cabin: $80-$160
Each additional person: $110
Children: Under 12, half price
*Higher price reflects two additional meals served.

Located two miles northwest of Pelican on the shores of Lisianski Inlet, the lodge is accessible only by boat or floatplane and its nearest neighbor is a half-mile away.

The main house is a log cabin built in 1939, which has been the Corbin's home since 1968. The bunkroom in the house sleeps four guests who share two bathrooms. The guest cabin, built in 1981, comes complete with kitchen and bathroom and sleeps up to five people.

The Corbins offer plenty to see and do in the area, including guided fishing trips in a 26-foot cruiser or extended tours on a 35-foot sailing ketch/power troller. They will also rent you a kayak or skiff or point the way to hiking trails and berry-picking spots. Glacier Bay is just two hours away by boat, White Sulphur Hot Springs is 45 minutes away by boat, and salmon or halibut fishing in the area is excellent.

Breakfast consists of sourdough pancakes, bacon and eggs, juice, coffee or tea. For an extra fee, all meals can be taken at the lodge. Those who rent the guest cabin do their own cooking.

"Lisianski Lodge will give you the feeling of living Alaska style. This homestead is in a remote area. Fishing for king salmon and halibut is the main pursuit, but berry pickers and mountain hikers can also find excellent activities here."

—Gail, Katie and Denny

OTTER COVE BED AND BREAKFAST

Box 618
Pelican, Alaska 99832
(907) 735-2259
Ginnie S. Porter and Chuck Piedra, Hosts

Months Open: February to November
Hours: 7 am to 11 pm
Credit Cards: None
Accommodations: One room
Children Welcome: All ages
Pets Accommodated: No
Social Drinking: Yes
Smoking: Outside

ROOM RATES
Single: $55   Double: $65
Each additional person: $10
Children: $10

The wooded path leading to Otter Cove Bed and Breakfast skirts terraced gardens full of flowers. In spring daffodils and tulips put on a marvelous display, and wildflowers such as chocolate lilies and columbines can be seen throughout the summer. The house is built over a small stream, and the highest tides come up under the front deck. The house has views of the inlet and rugged mountains beyond. Whales, sea otters, families of land otters, and birds such as kingfishers and great blue herons can often be seen from the house and deck.

The guest room is located at the rear of the house and is quite private. The room has built-in twin bunk beds and a queen-size futon for sitting or sleeping; a private guest bath with shower is close by. A back door leads to a secluded stream-side seating area. In late summer, salmonberry and blueberry bushes on both sides of the stream are loaded with fruit.

For breakfast, guests can expect fresh-baked wild berry coffeecake, zucchini frittata, fresh fruit, coffee and a choice of other beverage. Arrangements can be made for other meals; Ginnie charges $10 for lunch and about $15 for dinner, and will cook vegetarian, hearty, low-cal — guests' choice.

Pelican and the surrounding area, practically untouched

by tourism, have a lot to offer. Many local residents enjoy boating and fishing. There is an easy-to-follow trail, fishing charters, and kayak rental. Boat charters can also be arranged to nearby destinations, including White Sulfur Hot Springs.

OTTER COVE WILD BERRY COFFEECAKE

1/2 C butter
1/2 C brown sugar
1/2 C white sugar
2 eggs
1 1/2 t vanilla extract
2 C white flour
3/4 C buttermilk
1/2 t salt
1/2 t baking soda
1/2 t baking powder
1 1/2 C fresh wild berries
Topping (see ingredients below)

Cream butter and sugars. Add eggs and vanilla and set aside. Mix together flour, salt, baking soda, and baking powder. Alternate adding buttermilk and flour to egg mixture. Put berries in bottom of greased 9" x 13" stainless steel or glass pan. Gently pour batter over top.

Topping: Combine 1/2 C brown sugar, 1/2 C flour, 1/4 C butter and 1/2 t cinnamon; sprinkle over batter. Bake at 350 degrees for 45 minutes. Serve warm.

SITKA

On the west side of Baranof Island, 45 minutes from Juneau and two hours from Seattle, lies Sitka, population approximately 8,000. Set amid some of Southeast's most scenic surroundings, Sitka was originally a Tlingit Native village and later served as capital of Russian America. Today Sitka's residents make their livings commercial fishing, at jobs in the timber or tourism industries or with federal, state or local governments.

Visitor attractions in Sitka include:

◊ Saint Michael's Cathedral: This onion-domed church holds an outstanding collection of Russian Orthodox artifacts.

◊ Sheldon Jackson Museum: One of the finest collections of Native artwork in the state, much of it gathered by missionary Sheldon Jackson.

◊ New Archangel Dancers: Costumed folk dancers perform authentic Russian dances in the Centennial Building almost daily in summer.

◊ Alaska Day Festival: Commemorates the transfer of Alaska from Russia to the United States. Held October 15 through 18, the celebration includes a ball and local residents wearing period costumes.

◊ Russian Bishop's House: A log structure from Russian days, built in the 1840s for the Russian Orthodox Bishop, now stands as part of the Sitka National Historical Park.

◊ Sitka Summer Music Festival: Held each June, the festival features concerts on Tuesday and Friday evenings in the Centennial Building.

For more information contact:

Sitka Convention and Visitors Bureau
P.O. Box 1226
Sitka, Alaska 99835
(907) 747-5940

ALASKA OCEAN VIEW BED AND BREAKFAST

1101 Edgecumbe Drive
Sitka, Alaska 99835
(907) 747-8310; Fax (907) 747-8310
Bill and Carole Denkinger, Hosts

Months Open: Year-round
Hours. 21
Credit Cards: AMEX, MC, VISA
Accommodations: 3 rooms
Children Welcome: All ages
Pets Accommodated: No
Social Drinking: In rooms only
Smoking: Outdoors

ROOM RATES
Sitka Rose:
$69 single, $79 double (summer)
$59 single, $69 double (winter)
Fireweed:
$79 single, $89 double (summer)
$69 single, $79 double (winter)
Fireweed family rate: $99 (2 adults, 2 children)
Alaska Dogwood:
$99 single, $115 double (summer)
$89 single, $99 double (winter)
Each additional person: $15 (summer) $10 (winter)
(*Rates do not include 8% tax; all rates are cash discounted.)

Alaska Ocean View Bed and Breakfast is one block from the seashore and Tongass National Forest. It is within walking distance of the city center, harbor, trails, schools, shops and most attractions. Airport and ferry shuttle buses meet all jets and ferries, regardless of time, and deliver guests to Alaska Ocean View for less then $3.

Alaska Ocean View Bed and Breakfast is a three-story Alaska-style cedar home in a quiet neighborhood, offering ocean and mountain views, plenty of off-street parking and drive-up access to the first two floors. It is impeccably clean, cheerful

and tastefully decorated with local artists' work. There are large windows, a deck and a bubbling spa on the patio.

Three guest rooms named after Alaska wildflowers have private baths with showers, cable TV, VCR, phones, down comforters and writing tables. The Sitka Rose Room has a king-size bed and is decorated in wicker and brass. The Alaska Dogwood Room has a king-size bed, whirlpool tub with separate shower and ocean view. The Fireweed Room has two brass double beds, leather sofa sleeper, patio and private entrance. There is also a children's play area equipped with toys, books, videos and games nearby.

Breakfast offerings at Alaska Ocean View include fresh fruit in season, fresh-ground gourmet coffee and teas with a variety of flavored syrups and creamers, juice, cereal, fresh-baked bread, and entrees such as egg dishes, French toast, waffles, sourdough pancakes, bacon, sausage or quiche. Snacks are available in midafternoon and evening, including fresh-baked goodies (such as chocolate chip cookies) and microwave popcorn. Coffee, tea and hot chocolate are available 24 hours, along with any leftover breakfast items.

Sitka offers an abundance of things to see and do, including: historic sites, museums, Tlingit dancers, the state's Raptor Rehabilitation Center, Russian dancers, totem park, Russian Orthodox church, Russian bishop's house, trails, halibut and salmon fishing, kayak and boat rentals, bike rentals, ocean and wildlife sightseeing, wilderness flightseeing, land tours, whale and birdwatching and beachcombing. In June, the Sitka Summer Music Festival brings world-class musicians from around the globe to present concerts Tuesday and Friday evenings in the Centennial Building. The back wall of the Centennial Building's stage is glass and affords a panoramic view of salt water, islands, rugged snowcapped mountain peaks and soaring eagles — a magical treat of sight and sound.

BREAD-MAKER CINNAMON ROLLS, SITKA STYLE

3/4 C water
1 egg, beaten
3 C flour
6 T sugar
6 T butter, softened
2 T powdered milk
1 1/2 to 2 t rapid-rise yeast
1 t salt
butter, softened
2 t cinnamon
1/2 C sugar
raisins
half-and half

Place water and egg in automatic bread-maker bucket. Add the next six ingredients, in order listed.

Return bucket to maker and select "dough" setting. When beeper signals dough is ready, roll dough out on marble slab with marble rolling pin. Spread with softened butter, then sprinkle with mixture of cinnamon and sugar and raisins (optional). Roll up and cut into desired thickness and quantity. Place rolls in a buttered 9" x 13" baking pan sprinkled with brown sugar. Cover and set aside to rise overnight. Next morning, pour a little half-and-half over bottom of pan, just enough to cover the brown sugar but not over top of rolls. Bake uncovered at 350 degrees 30 minutes. Top with drizzle (see below). Serve warm! The brown sugar and half-and-half make a light caramel.

Drizzle: Blend powdered sugar with vanilla and a little milk to desired consistency.

CREEK'S EDGE GUEST HOUSE BED AND BREAKFAST

P.O. Box 2941
Sitka, Alaska 99835
(907) 747-6484
Jim and Bernadine McGinnis, Hosts

Months Open: Year-round
Hours: Flexible
Credit Cards: AMEX, MC, VISA
Accommodations: 3 rooms
Children Welcome: No
Pets Accommodated: No
Social Drinking: No
Smoking: No

ROOM RATES
Single or Double w/private bath: $95
Single w/shared bath: $55
Double w/shared bath: $65

Creek's Edge Guest House, about a mile-and-a-half out of town on Cascade Creek Road, is located on a site that offers truly spectacular views of Sitka Sound and Mount Edgecumbe.

Rooms at Creek's Edge are decorated with antiques and reproductions, with satin and lace accents reminiscent of days gone by. From the feather beds, topped with light comforters, guests can drift off to sleep to the sound of the nearby creek.

SOUTHCENTRAL ALASKA

Southcentral Alaska, the most populous region of the state, encompasses Anchorage, Alaska's largest city, and the well-populated Kenai Peninsula and Matanuska and Susitna valleys. Southcentral terrain varies, from the agricultural flatlands of the Matanuska Valley, to the rugged Chugach, Alaska and Kenai mountain ranges. The region is the home of several Native groups whose ancestors plied the productive waters of Cook Inlet, Prince William Sound, and Shelikof Strait in search of food and furs.

ANCHORAGE

Anchorage, Alaska's largest city, is the hub of Southcentral. Accessible by road, air and railroad, Anchorage is a metropolis where you can purchase almost anything you desire, from an extravagant gourmet meal to a beret hand-knit from arctic musk ox wool. You can see a play, watch the ballet, join a marathon race or visit a crafts fair...and the rest of Alaska is just minutes away.

There are literally hundreds of things for visitors to do in Anchorage, including:

◊ Anchorage Museum of History and Art: Located at the corner of 7th Avenue and 'A' Street, the museum features artwork by local, national and international artists, and offers permanent exhibits on Alaska history and Native culture.

◊ Alaska Zoo: See black, brown and polar bear, moose, musk ox, caribou, owls, fox, wolves, eagles and more, including elephants. Located on O'Malley Road in south Anchorage.

◊ Bicycle trails: More than 120 miles of paved bike trails are maintained in the Anchorage bowl and provide a delightful way to see the city's parks on foot as well as by bicycle. Bike rentals are available downtown, near the start of the coastal trail.

◊ Chugach State Park: Adjacent to Anchorage and accessible by trail from numerous points, the park provides almost 500,000 acres for hiking, climbing, camping, fishing and berry picking.

◊ Log Cabin Visitor Information Center: Located downtown at 4th Avenue and 'F' Street, the Log Cabin is an essential stop for visitors seeking maps, brochures and other information on Anchorage and surrounding areas.

◊ Alaska Railroad Depot: The railroad station, near downtown at Ship Creek, is the starting point for trips north to Mount McKinley and Fairbanks and south to Seward. The depot also has a display of historical photos from Anchorage's early "railroad town" days.

◊ Ship Creek Fish Ladder: This is the final hurdle at the end of an arduous journey from Cook Inlet to fresh water spawning grounds for chinook, coho and pink salmon. A viewing platform is located along the creek near the railroad station.

◊ Sporting events: In summer, visitors can watch local teams compete at slow-pitch softball on the downtown Delaney Park Strip, or they can attend amateur collegiate baseball games at Mulcahy Stadium. In winter, Anchorage is host to high school and college hockey games, the Great Alaska Shootout college invitational basketball tournament, and a variety of other winter sports, including sled dog racing.

◊ Potter Marsh State Game Refuge: Located about 10 miles south of downtown on the Seward Highway, Potter Marsh is an important nesting area for waterfowl. A variety of birds, including Canada geese, arctic terns, trumpeter swans and many species of ducks, can be viewed from the boardwalks built out over the marsh.

For more information, contact:

Anchorage Convention & Visitors Bureau
201 East Third Avenue
Anchorage, Alaska 99501
(907) 274-3531

A VIEW WITH A ROOM

8601 Sultana Drive
Anchorage, Alaska 99516
(907) 345-2781
Claire and Bob Young, Hosts

Months Open: Year-round
Hours: 5 pm to 11 am
Credit Cards: None
Accommodations: 3 rooms
Children Welcome: Over 12
Pets Accommodated: No
Social Drinking: Yes
Smoking: No

ROOM RATES
Single w/shared bath: $55
Double w/shared bath: $65
Loft w/private bath: $75
Each additional person: $10

A View with a Room, an easy 15-minute drive from Anchorage International Airport,overlooks the Anchorage Bowl, Turnagain Arm and Cook Inlet. Nearby is Chugach State Park and its many hiking trails.

Three comfortable rooms await guests at A View With A Room. The Chugach View room has a king-size bed that can be made into twins, and the Turnagain View room has a queen-size brass bed. Both rooms are decorated with antiques and "country-style decor." The new Anchorage Room is a loft with a private bath.

Breakfast is full or continental, including muffins, fruit plate, sourdough French toast, mushroom and cheese egg dishes, and a variety of other foods.

"We really do have a fantastic view...lots of moose and other wildlife, including birds that stop to rest. We hope to welcome you in our home on your visit to Anchorage."

—Claire and Bob

EASY BREAD PUDDING

4 slices bread, buttered and cubed
1 C brown sugar
Raisins (optional)
2 eggs, beaten
2 C milk
pinch salt
1 t vanilla

Place brown sugar in top of double boiler. Place bread cubes on top of sugar. Add raisins if desired. Mix eggs, milk, salt and vanilla. Pour this mixture over the bread. Do not stir. Cover and steam over low heat in double boiler for 1 1/2 hours. Serves 8. (Recipe is easy to double.)

ALASKAN FRONTIER GARDENS BED AND BREAKFAST

P.O. Box 241881
Anchorage, Alaska 99524-1881
(907) 345-6562 or (907) 345-6556
Fax (907) 562-2923
Rita Gittins, Hostess

Months Open: Year-round
Hours: 24
Credit Cards: VISA, MC
Accommodations: 3 rooms
Children Welcome: All ages
Pets Accommodated: Yes
Social Drinking: Yes
Smoking: Outside

ROOM RATES*
Ivory Suite:
Summer: $125 single; $175 double
Winter: $100 single; $150 double
Garden Terrace:
Summer: $100 single; $140 double
Winter: 85 single; $100 double
Fireweed Room:
Summer: $75 single; $100 double
Winter: $60 single; $75 double
(*Weekly and off-season rates are available)

An elegant, spacious home near Chugach State Park on Anchorage's peaceful Hillside, just 20 minutes from the airport and downtown, Alaskan Frontier Gardens is in a scenic wooded neighborhood at the corner of Hillside Drive and Alatna. Inside a wooden fence, the home sits nestled among trees, lawns and flowers. Alaska Frontier Gardens offers a museum-like atmosphere with Alaskan hospitality and exceptional comfort. Hostess Rita Gittins has lived in Alaska 30 years. Her active and well-traveled family enjoys many interesting hobbies, including hunting, fishing and sightseeing.

Rita offers guest parking in the garage, freezer space and

laundry facilities, and transportation can be arranged. Hiking, horseback riding, golfing, swimming or visiting the Alaska Zoo are just some of the things to do in this beautiful area of town, and the Gittins can provide recommendations for many other activities.

Alaskan Frontier Gardens' Ivory Suite includes a private bath, queen-size bed, fireplace, cable TV, VCR, sauna, large Jacuzzi, double shower, and a view of the city. The Garden Terrace Room has a private bath, king-size bed, television, VCR, and Jacuzzi with hanging plants. The Fireweed Room offers a spacious shared bath with a double and single beds and cable TV. Guests are welcome to use the barbecue grill. The Gittins' entire home is open for guests to use and enjoy, and it can accommodate wedding or anniversary parties of up to 200 people.

Breakfast delights include special recipe Belgian waffles or Amaretto French toast, reindeer sausage, fresh-ground gourmet coffee, tea, home-baked pastry, fresh fruit, hot and cold cereals, juice, and rum peaches.

"At our bed and breakfast, we feel our warm and friendly Alaskan hospitality and service is very important and probably is the reason we have many returning guests and personal references."

—Rita

ALL THE COMFORTS OF HOME

12531 Turk's Turn
Anchorage, Alaska 99516-3309
(907) 345-4279; Fax (907) 345-4761
Sydnee Mae Stiver, Hostess

Months Open: Year-round
Hours: 7 am to 9 pm
Credit Cards: AMEX, CB, DC, DS, MC, VISA
Accommodations: 3 rooms
Children Welcome: Well-behaved
Pets Accommodated: No
Social Drinking: Yes
Smoking: Outside

ROOM RATES*
Single: $60-$85
Double: $85-$125
Each additional person: $25
(*3-day minimum, May through September.)

All the Comforts of Home is located on five wooded acres at an elevation of 1,100 feet on Anchorage's Hillside. Volcanoes, glaciers, mountains and the city lights can all be seen from the property, and moose are frequent visitors.

The 12-room custom home was designed as a bed and breakfast. Each guest room is decorated with quality furnishings and functional antiques which hostess Sydnee, a life-long Alaskan, has collected during her extensive travels. All rooms have queen-size Beautyrest beds, down pillows and comforters, minifridges, TV-VCR and instant hot water taps. The Sourdough Suite offers a queen-size brass bed, TV, stereo, refrigerator, and Jacuzzi, and comes with the option of breakfast in bed. A secluded outdoor hot tub and wood-burning sauna add to the guests' enjoyment. There is also plenty of free parking, and freezer space is available for visitors' fish or game.

A hearty breakfast is served at All the Comforts of Home, starting with hot tea or fresh-ground coffee. Omelets, quiches, blintzes and other breakfast favorites are served each morning with juice, fresh fruit, hot breads, cereals, yogurt, and breakfast meats such as ham, Canadian bacon and reindeer sausage. Foods low in sugar, sodium and cholesterol are available for guests with special dietary requirements.

ARCTIC LOON BED AND BREAKFAST

P.O. Box 110333
Anchorage, Alaska 99511
Phone and Fax: (907) 345-4935
Janie and Lee Johnson, Hosts

Months Open: Year-round
Hours: 8 am to 11 pm
Credit Cards: MC, VISA
Accommodations: 3 rooms
Children Welcome: All ages
Pets Accommodated: No
Social Drinking: Yes
Smoking: Outside

ROOM RATES
Single: $60-$75 (summer) $50-$65 (winter)
Double: $70-$90 (summer) $65-$80 (winter)
Each additional person: $25
Children: $15 (under 5 free)

Arctic Loon Bed and Breakfast is located in the Hillside area of south Anchorage, 20 minutes from downtown or the airport, and just a few minutes from Chugach State Park hiking trails, the Alaska Zoo and a first-class golf course.

As a member of the prestigious American Bed and Breakfast Association (ABBA), Arctic Loon Bed and Breakfast has consistently received three-crown ratings after numerous yearly inspections by the organization. This rating designates that Arctic Loon Bed and Breakfast exceeds national standards met by less than 1 percent of the 20,000 B&Bs inspected by ABBA.

The Johnson's elegant 6,500-square foot home was designed by an award-winning architect to resemble a Swedish long house. Every room is situated to take advantage of the breathtaking views of the Anchorage Bowl, the Alaska Range, and Mount McKinley.

The three spacious guest rooms have TVs, phones, walk-in closets and spectacular views. Two rooms share a bath; the third has a private bath. The home features an eight-person hot tub, sauna, rosewood grand piano, exercise equipment, and pool table for guest use.

Guests can expect a full breakfast served in the Rosewood Room on English bone china. Breakfast features smoked salmon or reindeer sausage, fresh fruit and juice, muffins or croissants, gourmet hot dishes, cereal, milk, herbal teas, coffee or hot chocolate. Special diets can be accommodated on request.

Say the Johnsons, "At the Arctic Loon Bed and Breakfast, dedication to quality service and hospitality are key elements to our success." The large number of returning guests and word-of-mouth referrals provide evidence of their commitment.

ARCTIC PINES BED AND BREAKFAST

3310 Lois Drive
Anchorage, Alaska 99517
(907) 278-6841
Barbara and Matt Hall, Hosts

Months Open: Year-round
Hours: 9 am to 10 pm
Credit Cards: None
Accommodations: 3 rooms
Children Welcome: Age 3 and up
Pets Accommodated: By prior arrangement only
Social Drinking: Very moderate
Smoking: Outside in designated areas only

ROOM RATES
Shared bath: $65-$75   Private bath: $80-$90
Each additional person: $15
Winter rates: 10% off summer rates

Arctic Pines Bed and Breakfast is centrally located in midtown Anchorage. It is just minutes from the airport and downtown and is on the city bus route. Within two blocks, guests will find a 24-hour pharmacy, grocery store, dental and medical services, car rental, night clubs and restaurants.

Arctic Pines is a tri-level, cedar-sided home set back among trees, with flower-filled gardens and a hammock for relaxing. It offers three warm, comfortable rooms with access to a complete kitchen. One room has two twin beds (which can be converted to one king) and a private bath. The other two rooms have queen beds with in-room sink vanities and a shared bath.

Matt Hall grew up in Switzerland and France and has traveled extensively around the world. He is an expert skier. Barbara is interested in gardening and crafts.

A continental breakfast includes juice, tea, hot chocolate or coffee, with muffins, sweet rolls and fruit. A full, hearty breakfast includes bacon or sausage, eggs, hash browns, toast and cereal, with juice, tea, hot chocolate or coffee. Pancakes or waffles are offered for those who prefer them.

Lake Hood—the world's largest floatplane base, glacier and wildlife tours, parks and bike trails are all nearby.

BONNIE'S BED AND BREAKFAST

8501 Upper Huffman
Anchorage, Alaska 99516
(907) 345-4671
Darrell and Ruby Hill, Hosts

Months Open: Year-round
Hours: 9 am to 9 pm
Credit Cards: None
Accommodations: 2 rooms
Children Welcome: Over 12
Pets Accommodated: No
Social Drinking: No
Smoking: No

ROOM RATES
Single: $50
Double: $60
Each additional person: $10

Bonnie's Bed and Breakfast, situated on a bluff at the top of Upper Huffman Road in south Anchorage, has a bird's-eye view of Anchorage and Cook Inlet and Mount McKinley beyond. The home has two guest bedrooms, which share a bath. One room has twin beds; the other has a queen-size bed. Amenities include a small sitting room with TV and VCR for guests, and telephones in each guest room. Bonnie's Bed and Breakfast is an easy 20-minute drive from the airport or downtown.

The Hills enjoy hunting, fishing and camping in their spare time.

"At Bonnie's Bed and Breakfast we feature a full breakfast along with a beautiful view..."

—Darrell and Ruby

CAMAI BED AND BREAKFAST

3838 Westminster Way
Anchorage, Alaska 99508-4834
(907) 333-2219 or (800) 659-8763
Caroline and Craig Valentine, Hosts

Months Open: Year-round
Hours: Check in after 3 pm; check out by 11 am
Credit Cards: None
Accommodations: 2 suites
Children Welcome: All ages
Pets Accommodated: No
Social Drinking: Yes
Smoking: No

ROOM RATES
1 night only:
Single: $85 (summer) $70 (winter)
Double: $95 (summer) $75 (winter)
2+ consecutive nights:
Single: $65 (summer) $50 (winter)
Double: $75 (summer) $55 (winter)
Each additional person: $10

Camai (pronounced cha-my) means "warm Alaskan hello," and that's just what you'll get from Caroline and Craig Valentine. Caroline is a math teacher and church organist; Craig is a civil engineer. Many summer vegetables and flowers enhance this traditional-style home located in a quiet east Anchorage neighborhood. A stream borders the large property, which is near parks, two universities and shopping.

Camai offers two suites. The Rosewood Suite has a queen-size rosewood bed in the bedroom, a daybed (which converts to two single beds) in the solar room, a private bath, dressing room and deck. The Teak Suite has a queen-size teak bed, its own sitting room with daybed, a private bath and kitchenette, and is handicapped accessible. Both suites have private entries.

The Valentines serve a breakfast with fresh fruit, waffles, pancakes, French toast topped with maple syrup, or healthy cheese and broccoli strata, juice, fresh-ground coffee, tea and milk.

HEALTHY CHEESE AND BROCCOLI STRATA

2 1/2 C (4 slices) bread cubes
12 oz Cheddar-like skim milk cheese product
2 C broccoli flowerets
1/4 C melted margarine
1/2 lb sliced fresh mushrooms
16 oz egg substitute
1 1/2 C nonfat milk
1 tsp Chinese style, extra-hot prepared mustard

Place half the bread cubes in a 1 1/2-quart casserole. Layer half the broccoli, half the cheese, then the remaining bread cubes. Pour half the margarine over top; repeat layering with remaining half of broccoli, cheese and margarine. Top with mushrooms. Mix egg substitute, milk and mustard. Pour over layers in casserole. Bake at 300 degrees for 1 1/4 hours, or until top is lightly browned.

COUNTRY GARDEN
BED AND BREAKFAST

8210 Frank Street
Anchorage, Alaska 99518
(907) 344-0636
Kay and Jim Heafner, Hosts

Months Open: Year-round
Hours: 8 am to 11 pm
Credit Cards: None
Accommodations: 3 rooms
Children Welcome: Yes
Pets Accommodated: No
Social Drinking: No
Smoking: No

ROOM RATES
Single: $60 (summer) $50 (winter)
Double: $80 (summer) $70 (winter)
Each additional person: $15 (summer) $10 (winter)
Children: $15

Country Garden Bed and Breakfast is a small, uniquely warm and friendly bed and breakfast owned and operated by a long-time Alaskan couple. Throughout the house, antiques and hand-stenciled walls mix tastefully with casual country decor. Fresh flowers, cut daily from abundantly blooming flower gardens, decorate the house and bedrooms. The beautifully landscaped yard, in its wooded setting, received rave reviews on the 1990 Anchorage Garden Tour.

Country Garden Bed and Breakfast offers three guest rooms. The Mountain View Room has a queen-size canopy bed and a balcony. The Hudson Bay Room has twin beds and the Outfitter Room has a single bed. Bathrooms, with a king-size tub and double shower, are shared.

Country Gardens' hosts have a great fondness for Alaska and are very knowledgeable about the surrounding countryside. Jim is an avid fly-fisherman and may be coaxed into sharing some of his favorite fly patterns. Kay's warm hospitality and her love of flowers, gardening and catering graciously accent this charming bed and breakfast.

A full country breakfast made up of Dutch apple pancakes or sugar-top blueberry muffins, ham, fresh melon and berries, eggs and homemade breads will lure you from your bed. An evening dessert is included with coffee and tea!

DE VEAUX'S CONTEMPORARY BED AND BREAKFAST

4011 Iona Circle
Anchorage, Alaska 99507
(907) 349-8910
Robert and Mary De Voue, Hosts

Months Open: April through September
Hours: 7 am to 12 pm
Credit Cards: None
Accommodations: 3 rooms
Children Welcome: All ages
Pets Accommodated: No
Social Drinking: Yes
Smoking: No

ROOM RATES
Single: $65 and $85
Double: $75 and $95

DeVeaux's Contemporary Bed and Breakfast is a tri-level house located south of Anchorage on a quiet rolling-hill, country site with a spectacular view of the mountains on all sides. It is mere minutes from the airport, museum, restaurants, gyms, zoo, equestrian trails, golf course, ski areas, universities and hospitals.

Bob and Mary are long-time Alaskans and travelers who love meeting people, reading, decorating, fine arts and music.

DeVeaux's has upper and lower decks off the dining area and family room. Both decks are decorated with flowers. A barbecue grill is available. The bed and breakfast is decorated in gray, burgundy and shades of rose and pink with teal accents. The Pennsylvania Room has a classic decor with a queen-size brass bed, cherry wood dresser, lots of flowers and lace. It has a view of Mount McKinley. The New York Room is ultramodern, with black lacquer furniture and brass accents. Its private bath has a whirlpool tub and double sinks. The Arizona Room has a double bed, white ash furniture and a southwestern decor in navy blue, teal, rose and off-white. It has a view of the Chugach Mountains.

A typical breakfast includes wholewheat buttermilk Belgium waffles with various syrups, fruit, ham, bacon or sausages, eggs, juice, coffee made from fresh-ground beans, and tea. Complimentary snacks are available.

CALYPSO EGGS

1 T margarine or butter
1/4 C chopped red or green bell pepper
2 T sliced green onions
1/2 C low-fat cottage cheese
2 drops hot pepper sauce
dash of salt
dash of pepper
3 eggs, beaten

Melt margarine in medium skillet over medium heat. Add chopped peppers and onions; cook and stir until tender. In small bowl, combine remaining ingredients; add to vegetable mixture. Cook over medium heat until eggs are thoroughly cooked, stirring occasionally. Makes two servings.

ELDERBERRY BED AND BREAKFAST

8340 Elderberry
Anchorage, Alaska 99502
(907) 243-6968
Norm and Linda Seitz, Hosts

Months Open: Year-round
Hours: 24
Credit Cards: MC, VISA
Accommodations: 3 rooms
Children Welcome: All ages
Pets Accommodated: Yes
Social Drinking: Yes
Smoking: On deck

ROOM RATES
Summer: Starting from $65
Winter: Starting from $50

Close to the airport and bike and walking trails, Elderberry Bed and Breakfast is in the Sand Lake area of Anchorage. It is near the bus route and within walking distance of several popular restaurants. The Seitz's home is a comfortable, two-story yellow house with Early American furnishings. Linda and Norm take special pride in their yard and flowers in the summer. (Linda has won blue ribbons in flower shows.) Often moose can be spotted from the large viewing windows in their sun room.

There are three guest rooms. One has a double bed and private bath across the hall, decorated in Victorian pale green and rose. Another room, decorated in green and white wild-flower design, has a queen-size bed with a shower in the room. The third room is decorated in red, white and blue nautical design, and has twin beds and a shared bath.

Guests are welcome throughout the main level of the home and may choose to sit by the fireplace in the sitting room and read Alaskan books. Guests are also welcome in the sun room to sit by the wood stove and watch videos or TV, enjoy the 45-inch surround-sound stereo, or chat. Both Norm and Linda have lived in Alaska since 1977 and love to meet new people and share their Alaskan experiences with them. Linda considers Norm one of their most popular attractions, as he loves to talk with the guests.

Linda and Norm will cater to your needs and will try to fill any request, from a special diet to parking for your RV (they provide parking space, complete with electricity and water hookups). They will provide freezer space for your catch as well as a TV in your room.

Guests are offered many choices for breakfast, such as oven omelettes and quiches. Fresh fruit is served daily, as well as muffins, bagels, donuts, juice and teas. Fresh, hot homemade bread is also offered. Linda's specialty is her homemade strawberry jam. Gourmet coffee is served on request.

ENGLISH COUNTRY BED AND BREAKFAST

2911 Rocky Bay Circle
Anchorage, Alaska 99515
(907) 344-0646
Bill and Debbie Jaso, Hosts

Months Open: Year-round
Hours: 8 am to 10 pm
Credit Cards: None
Accommodations: 1 room
Children Welcome: Over 12
Pets Accommodated: No
Social Drinking: Yes
Smoking: No

ROOM RATES
Single: $70 (summer) $65 (winter)
Double: $85 (summer) $75 (winter)
Each additional person: $15
Children over 12: $15

English Country Bed and Breakfast, located in south Anchorage about 10 minutes from the airport, offers exceptional comfort amidst a charming, elegant country decor.

Debbie is a caterer, gardener and interior decorator who grew up in Sitka. Bill loves to ski, mountain bike and hike. When he came to visit Alaska in 1974, he felt he'd found his home. He is also interested in photography and cooking.

English Country's special amenities include a clawfoot bathtub and evening appetizers. The guest room offers a queen-size bed and a private bath.

A full breakfast is included, consisting of fruit juice, coffee, fruit plate, homemade muffins, frittata, waffles, pancakes or omelette, reindeer sausage or ham.

English Country B&B is near tennis courts, a running track and bike trails, and within a short distance of Anchorage tours, Kincaid Park, Potter Marsh bird-viewing area, Turnagain Arm, shopping malls and the Anchorage Museum.

APPLE PECAN MUFFINS

1 C sifted flour
1 t baking powder
1/4 t salt
5 T sugar
1/2 t ground cinnamon
1 egg, beaten
2 T melted butter
1/3 C milk
1/2 C apples, cored, peeled and chopped
2 heaping T chopped pecans
2 T sugar mixed with a dash of ground cinnamon

Sift flour with baking powder, salt, sugar and cinnamon.
Set aside. Combine egg, melted butter and milk. Stir lightly into
flour mixture. (Do not mix to satin-smooth consistency—lumps
in batter are fine.) Stir in apples and pecans. Fill greased muffin
cups two-thirds full and dust with sugar/cinnamon mixture.
Bake at 400 degrees 15 to 20 minutes. Remove from oven and
let stand 2 to 3 minutes for easy removal. Serve immediately.
Makes 12 muffins.

GLACIER BEAR BED AND BREAKFAST

4814 Malibu Road
Anchorage, Alaska 99517
(907) 243-8818; Fax (907) 248-4532
Keith and Georgia Taton, Marge Brown, Hosts

Months Open: Year-round
Hours: 7 am to 11 pm
Credit Cards: MC, VISA
Accommodations: 5 rooms
Children Welcome: Over 12
Pets Accommodated: No
Social Drinking: Yes
Smoking: Outside

ROOM RATES*
Queen/king rooms: $89
Twin room: $79
Rollaway: $20
(*Summer rates are shown; call for winter rates.)

Located 1.2 miles from the airport and only blocks from the world's largest float plane lake, the Glacier Bear Bed and Breakfast provides first class accommodation in a parklike setting. A courtesy van provides airport service for arrivals and departures. The contemporary, 5,000-square-foot home is cedar-sided with lots of windows and beautiful landscaping.

Throughout the house, guests will find a mixture of Oriental and Victorian accents; one of the bedrooms has a pencil canopy bed while another bedroom contains an antique king-size bed and fireplace.

Hosts Keith and Georgia Taton have traveled the world and lived for many years on a tropical island in the Pacific. They love to meet new people from the world over and understand the wants of all travelers, whether their trips are business or pleasure. Marge Brown is a recognized craftsman and her works of art can be seen throughout the home.

Guests at Glacier Bear have a choice of a full or continental breakfasts, which include large fresh muffins, fruit, juice and fresh-ground gourmet coffee or tea served at the dining table in the common area.

GLACIER BEAR CINNAMON ROLLS

3/4 C milk
1 pkg dry yeast
1 egg
1/3 C sugar
1/4 C melted shortening
1 t salt
3 C flour

Bring milk to a boil, then cool to lukewarm. Dissolve yeast in 1/4 C warm water. Mix milk and yeast mixture with other ingredient. Place dough in greased bowl and allow to rise for 1 1/2 hours, then knead on a lightly floured board. Let rise again for 30 minutes. Roll out, spread with melted butter and sprinkle with a cinnamon and sugar mixture. Roll up and cut into 1-inch slices. Place cut side down in pan and cover with a thick mixture of melted butter, brown sugar and milk. Bake at 350 degrees for approximately 15 to 20 minutes.

HEIDI'S BED AND BREAKFAST

3904 Lois Drive
Anchorage, Alaska 99517-2651
(907) 563-8517
Heidi and John McLane, Hosts

Months Open: Year-round
Hours: 24
Credit Cards: None
Accommodations: 2 bedroom apartment
Children Welcome: All ages
Pets Accommodated: On approval
Social Drinking: Yes
Smoking: Outside

ROOM RATES
Single: $55 (summer) $45 (winter)
Double: $60 (summer) $50 (winter)

Heidi's Bed and Breakfast is a two-bedroom apartment attached to the hosts' home, centrally located five minutes from Anchorage International Airport and downtown. It is two blocks from a car rental agency, bus depot and cafe.

The two-story apartment has off-street parking, a fenced yard, modest but comfortable furniture, and a kitchenette. Both bedrooms are upstairs; one, a double room with blue decor, and across the hall, a twin room with rose decor. The living area has a queen-size sofa sleeper.

Heidi is a 16-year resident of Anchorage who works part time for the University of Alaska. John, a journeyman electrician, works for the Anchorage School District and has lived in Alaska for 20 years.

A delicious breakfast of sourdough rolls or breads, low-fat granola, fresh fruit, fresh-ground coffee, tea, cocoa and hot spiced cider is offered. Hot beverages are available for guests at all times.

SOURDOUGH HAM AND CHEESE ROLLS

5 1/2 to 6 1/2 C flour
    (half whole-wheat, half unbleached white)
1/4 C sugar
1 t salt
2 pkgs dry yeast
1/2 C Canola oil or margarine
1 C warm water
1/2 C sourdough starter
2 eggs
1/2 C cream cheese, softened
1 1/2 C chopped ham
1 C sharp Cheddar cheese, grated

In large bowl, mix 1 1/2 C flour, sugar, salt, dry yeast and oil or margarine. Mix warm water and sourdough starter; gradually add to flour mixture. Beat for two minutes at medium speed, scraping bowl as needed. Add 1/4 C flour and eggs. Beat at high speed for two minutes. By hand, add the rest of the flour and make a soft dough. Knead five minutes. Roll out on floured board and shape into a 14" x 9" rectangle. Spread dough with cream cheese, then sprinkle on the chopped ham and Cheddar cheese (green onions may also be added). Roll up dough, pinch edges to seal, and cut into 1-inch slices. Oil a 9" x14" pan. Arrange rolls on pan. Keep in warm place until double in size. Bake at 350 degrees 20 minutes. Serve warm with coffee and fruit salad.

LITTLE RABBIT CREEK BED AND BREAKFAST

5420 Rabbit Creek Road
Anchorage, Alaska 99516-4906
Phone and Fax: (907) 345-8183
Cal and Cathy Powers, Hosts

Months Open: Year-round
Hours: 6 am to 10 pm
Credit Cards: MC, VISA
Accommodations: 2 rooms
Children Welcome: Well-behaved, 6 years and older
Pets Accommodated: No
Social Drinking: Yes
Smoking: Outdoors only

ROOM RATES*
Single: $70
Double: $80
Each additional person: $25
(maximum 2 additional persons per room)
Children: $10 (maximum 2 per room)
*Minimum 2-night stay from May to September

Little Rabbit Creek Bed and Breakfast is located on Anchorage's wooded hillside, next to a beautiful creek just 15 scenic minutes from the airport and 20 minutes from downtown. It is a new home, with more than 1,000 square feet devoted to the bed and breakfast guest level. Interesting antiques and Alaska art fill the home, and it was constructed in a way that takes advantage of the creek view and blends with the surrounding forest.

The Creekside Room has a wonderful oak antique bed with queen-size mattress, mirrored wash stand, comfortable wing-back chair, dining table, TV and private full bath. Guests can listen to and look at the creek through lace curtains—it is only 30 feet from the large window. There is also space to use futon beds for two extra in-room guests.

The Wild Rabbit Suite consists of a bedroom and a sitting room. It features a brass and iron bed with a queen-size mattress, antique oak dresser, double futon couch, dining table, TV and private full bath. Wild rabbits roam in the nearby meadow, visible through a sitting room window. The futon couch can be converted to a double bed to accommodate two extra in-room guests.

The guest lobby includes an antique wood stove, railroad bench, library table, small refrigerator for guest use and telephone. There is also an outside deck where guests can enjoy watching birds, rabbits and moose and sharing stories of their travels.

Cal has been in Alaska since 1975 when he joined the "great Alaska pipeline boom." He continues to work for a major oil company and uses his free time to hunt, fish and camp throughout Alaska with his family. Cathy has worked as a teacher, art consultant and homemaker. She loves to share her love of Alaska with guests.

Breakfast is served in the great room overlooking the creek and may be either a generous, Alaska-style continental or a full breakfast including freshly baked goods, juice, fresh fruit and daily specials such as sourdough pancakes, crepes or omelettes. On occasion, Cathy makes cookies and "mango" tea to share with guests.

Nearby, visitors will find Chugach State Park, hiking trails, golf course, Alaska Zoo, local Nordic and Alpine ski areas, Potter Marsh, great shopping malls and restaurants.

JOHN WAYNE'S FAVORITE RECIPE

1 lg loaf sandwich bread, sourdough French bread or
    corn bread, thickly sliced (make sure the bread is not
    the light, airy type or it will tear)
butter or margarine
1 lg can of chopped Ortega chilies
1/2 lb Cheddar cheese, shredded
1/2 lb Jack cheese or hot pepper Jack cheese, shredded
5 eggs
3 C milk

Trim crusts from bread. Butter one side of slices and place
half of the bread, buttered side down in a 9"x13" baking dish
sprayed with vegetable cooking spray. Place chopped chilies
over bread. Sprinkle with half of the two cheeses. Top with
remaining bread slices, buttered side up. Mix beaten eggs and
milk together and pour over the bread. Sprinkle remaining
cheese over top and sprinkle with dried parsley. Cover with
plastic wrap and refrigerate overnight. In the morning, bake at
350 degrees until puffed up and set, about 45 minutes or until
knife inserted in center comes out clean. It should come out of
the oven puffed up and golden brown like a souffle. Letting it
set up for 5 to 10 minutes will make it much easier to cut and
serve. May be served with salsa, guacamole and/or sour cream.
Serves 10.

LYNN'S PINE POINT BED AND BREAKFAST

3333 Creekside Drive
Anchorage, Alaska 99504
(907) 333-2244
Richard and Lynnette Stouff, Hosts

Months Open: Year-round
Hours: 8 am to 10 pm
Credit Cards: MC, VISA
Accommodations: 3 rooms
Children Welcome: Yes
Pets Accommodated: No
Social Drinking: Yes
Smoking: On porch

ROOM RATES
Single: $75 (summer) $65 (winter)
Double: $85 (summer) $75 (winter)
Each additional person: $20

Lynn's Pine Point Bed and Breakfast is a cedar retreat amid birch and pine trees. It is beautifully decorated, furnished with antiques, and has a lovely landscaped yard. A gazebo sits amid this natural setting, where guests can relax and enjoy the cocktails and hors d'oeuvres which are served on arrival.

Lynn's provides more than 500 video movies, microwaves, snacks and a view of the Chugach mountains. Each room has a color TV and VCR. There are tennis courts and a physical fitness/bike trail at the end of the road for those who want to include a little exercise in their vacation.

Breakfast, served between 6 a.m. and 9 a.m., changes regularly, but includes fresh ground coffee, pancakes, sausage, bacon, French toast or eggs, homemade muffins, fruit, and juice. After breakfast, a short drive will take you to the Alaska Zoo, the Anchorage Museum, Hatcher Pass or the state fairgrounds at Palmer.

PINE POINT RHUBARB CRUNCH

Topping:
   1 C flour
   3/4 C rolled oats
   1 C brown sugar
   1 t cinnamon
   1/2 C melted butter
Filling:
   1 C sugar
   2 T corn starch
   1 C water
   1 t vanilla
   4 C diced rhubarb

Butter an 8" x 8" pan (9" x 13" pan if you double ingredients). Mix topping ingredients well and pack half the mixture in bottom of pan. Combine all filling ingredients except rhubarb in a saucepan. Heat until mixture is thick and clear. Pack the rhubarb into a baking pan; pour filling mixture over. Cover with remaining topping and bake at 350 degrees for 1 hour. (Note: This will bubble over, so put a cookie sheet or foil under it.)

MULLEN HOUSE BED AND BREAKFAST

1511 'I' Street
Anchorage, Alaska 99501
Evenings: (907) 258-9260 Days: (907) 562-4155
Fax: (907) 563-2891
Mary Mullen, Hostess

Months Open: Year-round
Hours: 24
Credit Cards: None
Accommodations: 2 rooms
Children Welcome: All ages
Pets Accommodated: No
Social Drinking: Yes
Smoking: Outside in the garden

ROOM RATES
Single: $50   Double: $70
Children: $10
(Summer rates are given; winter rates are negotiable.)

Mullen House Bed and Breakfast is a 1940s home in one of Anchorage's oldest neighborhoods, a 10-minute walk from downtown and just 10 minutes by car from the airport.

This white and blue "grandma's house" has a pitched roof which makes the upstairs cozy. Irish lace curtains and fresh flowers grace the kitchen, and the sheets are line dried to smell fresh and clean. The main-floor bedroom has one queen-size bed and a private bathroom with tub, shower and cheery wallpaper. This is a good room for those who can't climb stairs. The second-floor room has one queen-size bed and one twin, and shares a bathroom with Mary. The decor throughout the home is feminine, with nice carpeting, artwork and antiques.

Mary, a born-and-raised Alaskan who works in the health and social services field, describes herself as a woman who "likes to travel and enjoys making single people comfortable in a world which mostly caters to couples." Her other interests include Alaska history, walking, photography, politics, writing and sharing Anchorage's pleasant things, such as the arts.

Breakfast at Mullen House consists of fruit, cereal, yogurt, fresh-baked goods and coffee. Popcorn is offered at night.

SNOWLINE BED AND BREAKFAST

**11101 Snowline Drive
Anchorage, Alaska 99516
(907) 346-1631
Ed and Dana Klinkhart, Hosts**

Months Open: Year-round
Hours: 24
Credit Cards: MC, VISA
Accommodations: 2 rooms
Children Welcome: Yes
Pets Accommodated: No
Social Drinking: Yes
Smoking: Designated outside area

ROOM RATES
Susitna Room: $85
Denali Room: $105
Each additional person: $15
(Rates are based on double occupancy.)

Snowline Bed and Breakfast is in a three-story A-frame home located in the quiet Hillside area just 20 minutes from the airport and downtown Anchorage. An attached greenhouse provides flowers that adorn the deck and yard. Snowline has been inspected, rated and approved by the American Bed and Breakfast Association.

The Susitna Room is a suite with king-size bed, sitting room, private bath, color TV and a library of Alaskan books. The Denali Room has over 500 square feet of living space with a magnificent view, private entrance, queen-size bed, color TV, VCR, refrigerator, table and chairs, video library and private six-person Jacuzzi.

A telescope is available to enhance the views of Anchorage, Cook Inlet, and Mount McKinley from the living room or sun deck. Chugach State Park, hiking trails, a golf course and the Alaska Zoo are just minutes away. Snowline is less than five minutes from popular winter Nordic and Alpine ski areas.

A continental breakfast features such treats as Dana's homemade cinnamon rolls and sourdough muffins. Fresh-ground coffee is always on early.

SNOWLINE ICED TEA SYRUP

3 C boiling water
1/2 C loose tea
2 C sugar
1/4 t baking soda

Pour boiling water over loose tea and allow to steep for five minutes. Strain tea and add sugar and soda. Stir to dissolve and store in refrigerator. Pour over ice cubes and add water to desired strength. Add lemon, if desired.

SWAN HOUSE BED AND BREAKFAST

6840 Crooked Tree Drive
Anchorage, Alaska 99516
(907) 346-3033, (800) 921-1900; Fax: (907) 346-3535
Judy and Jerry Swanson, Hosts

Months Open: Year-round
Hours: 6 am to 10 pm
Credit Cards: AMEX, DS, MC, VISA
Accommodations: 2 rooms
Children Welcome: No
Pets Accommodated: No
Social Drinking: Yes
Smoking: No

ROOM RATES
Single: $115 (summer) $80 (winter)
Double: $135 (summer) $100 (winter)

Swan House Bed and Breakfast overlooks the city of Anchorage, with a view of Mount McKinley in the background. It is in a quiet, hillside neighborhood with lots of trees and moose, 15 minutes from town or the airport.

Swan House is architecturally unique, with 127 windows and more exposed wood than is normally seen in a home. The exterior is heartwood redwood, and oak dominates the interior with a black walnut and Corian fireplace. Corian is in every room, along with antiques from all over the world. The home has been the setting for numerous weddings and honeymoons.

Swan House has two guest rooms with private baths, one with queen-size bed, and one with king-size bed or two twin beds. Both rooms have cable TVs and phones.

Jerry and Judy are employed by the Federal Aviation Administration. They are both pilots and enjoy fishing, flying and skiing.

Guests may expect full gourmet breakfasts with fruit smoothies, fresh-ground coffee and tea. Beverages are available any time.

Area activities include hiking, biking, cross-country and downhill skiing and golfing (one mile from the house).

VALLEY OF THE MOON
BED AND BREAKFAST

1578 'E' Street
Anchorage, Alaska 99501
(907) 279-7755
Ed and Kee Miner, Hosts

Months Open: Year-round
Hours: 7:20 am to 10:30 pm
Credit Cards: None
Accommodations: 3 rooms
Children Welcome: All ages
Pets Accommodated: No
Social Drinking: Yes
Smoking: On outdoor deck

ROOM RATES
Single: w/shared bath, $65; w/private bath, $75
Double: w/shared bath, $75; w/private bath, $85
(Summer rates are given; winter rates are $20-$30 lower.)

Valley of the Moon Bed and Breakfast is ideally located for people who appreciate the convenience of being downtown and enjoy walking or biking to the city's attractions. This home, located just 10 blocks from the heart of Anchorage, offers welcome views of the Chugach Mountains and easy access to Anchorage's popular coastal trail. Two 18-speed mountain bikes and a five-speed tandem are available to adventurous guests who wish to explore the city and restore their travel-weary spirits.

The Miner family, hosts of Valley of the Moon, has devoted itself to Alaska visitors for more than five years. Their experience shows in the thoughtful way they provide for their guests' comfort and needs. Accommodations include three attractive bedrooms. The master bedroom has a private bath, a queen-size bed and a small sleeper-sofa. The other two rooms share a bath; one has a queen-size bed, the other has twin beds (these can be converted to a king-size bed on request). The handsomely furnished living and dining rooms are for guests' exclusive use (the Miners live upstairs). The family's collection of contemporary Alaska art highlights their home, and brilliantly colored flower beds abound on the well-tended property.

Breakfast is "hearty continental" with hot, homemade bread, fresh-baked scones or muffins, cut fruit, jams, coffees and teas. Everything is prepared the evening before, so that guests can eat breakfast whenever they wish.

CRANBERRY SCONES

2/3 C buttermilk or lemon yogurt
1 large egg
3 C all-purpose flour
4 t baking powder
1/2 t baking soda
1/2 t salt
8 T cold, unsalted butter, cut into pieces
3/4 C fresh or frozen cranberries, coarsely chopped
1/2 C granulated sugar
1 t freshly grated orange peel

Preheat oven to 375 degrees. Measure buttermilk or yogurt into a 2-cup glass measure; beat in egg with a fork. Combine flour, baking powder, baking soda and salt in a large bowl. Stir to mix well. Cut butter into flour mixture with a pastry cutter until the mixture resembles coarse meal (a food processor may also be used). Toss cranberries, sugar and orange peel together and add to flour mixture. Add buttermilk and egg. Stir with a fork until a soft dough forms.

Turn out dough onto a lightly floured board and knead lightly, just until well mixed. Divide dough in half and form each piece into a ball, then pat into two circles on ungreased baking sheet. Cut each circle into 8 wedges with a serrated knife. Bake for 18 to 20 minutes, or until the top is lightly browned and the center is no longer sticky. Cool in pan on a wire rack for 5 minutesbefore transferring scones to the wire rack with a spatula. Recut wedges if necessary.

COOPER LANDING

Located about 100 miles south of Anchorage on the Kenai Peninsula, Cooper Landing stretches along several miles of the Sterling Highway. Visitor facilities are convenient and plentiful, offering travelers a much-needed leg-stretching break when motoring up or down the Kenai Peninsula. The Kenai River skirts town and provides a variety of recreational opportunities, which help make Cooper Landing a desirable destination. Raft trips, mountain trails, fishing and sighseeing are just a few of the many activities available.

RED SALMON GUEST HOUSE

P.O. Box 725
Cooper Landing, Alaska 99572
(907) 595-1733, (800) 595-8687; Fax: (907) 595-1533
Patti and George Heim, Hosts

Months Open: May to October
Hours: 24
Credit Cards: MC, VISA
Accommodations: 2 rooms, 3 cabins, 1 suite
Children Welcome: All ages
Pets Accommodated: Inquire
Social Drinking: Yes
Smoking: No

ROOM RATES
Single: $79 to $99
Double: $99 to $199
Each additional person: $20
Children Under 11: Free (in room with parent)

Red Salmon Guest House is located in picturesque Cooper Landing, 100 miles south of Anchorage, on the banks of the upper Kenai River, famous for its wild salmon. The guest house is convenient to all points on the Kenai Peninsula. Wildlife such as sheep, moose and eagles abounds in the area.

George has one of only 20 permits issued to take clients fishing within the Kenai National Wildlife Refuge. Patti, who loves to travel, runs an on-site travel agency.

Two upstairs rooms in the guest house share a bath, semi-private entrance and deck; downstairs is a two-bedroom suite with private bath. The three Alaska cabins have private baths. All feature good views of the river. World-class fishing, wonderful day hikes to Exit Glacier and Russian River Falls, and scenic river rafting trips are available from the guest house. Tourist information, a collection of videos, in-room TVs, a library, espresso bar, and a freezer for fish are also available at Red Salmon Guest House.

Guests gather for a full breakfast in the beautiful dining room overlooking the river. The menu includes gourmet coffee, espresso, fresh orange juice, reindeer sausage, blueberry pancakes with Alaska syrup, country fried potatoes and the sweet of the day.

CORDOVA

Fishing is Cordova's lifeblood. The community hums around-the-clock with activity insummer but grows quieter in winter when fishing slows down.A controversial road to connect Cordova with the road system has yet to be built, but the town welcomes visitors by air or ferry.

Visitor attractions in Cordova include:

◊ Iceworm Festival: Held the first weekend in February with a 100-foot worm-led parade, beard judging contest and King and Queen.

◊ Silver Salmon Derby: During the last weekend of August and first weekend of September anglers compete for the biggest fish and prizes.

◊ Cordova Museum and Library: A plaque explains the archaeological significance of this site on Hawkins Island, where Chugach Eskimos lived 4,000 years ago.

For more information contact:

Cordova Chamber of Commerce
Box 99
Cordova, Alaska 99574
(907) 424-7260

CORDOVA ROSE LODGE

P.O. Box 1494
Cordova, Alaska 99574
(907) 424-Rose (7673)
Eldon and Jan Glein, Hosts

Months Open: Year-round
Hours: 6 am to 1 am
Credit Cards: MC, VISA
Accommodations: 5 rooms
Children Welcome: All ages
Pets Accommodated: No
Social Drinking: Yes
Smoking: No

ROOM RATES
Single w/private shower: $65 (summer) $60 (winter)
Single w/shared shower: $55 (summer) $50 (winter)
Each additional person: $10
Children 8 and under: Free in room with parents

Cordova Rose Lodge is a retrofitted barge that was built in 1924 in Kodiak. The barge has a colorful history, having served in the Gulf of Alaska as a fish trap setter, cannery, machine shop, living quarters for a recluse and houseboat. Today, as a bed and breakfast lodge, it is a Cordova landmark.

Owners Eldon and Jan Glein remodeled the landlocked barge, creating comfortable quarters with a nautical theme. Captain Eldon is a retired Navy man, hunter, fisherman, and photographer; Chief Mate Jan is "chief cook and bottle washer."

The grounds are landscaped with a myriad of wild and domestic flowers and plants, and offer a gazebo. A U.S. Coast Guard certified lighthouse shines a beacon at night. Cordova Rose Lodge offers its guests a library, cable TV, woodstove, microwave, refrigerator, a breakwater with bridges, and an observation deck with a view of the city harbor. One room has a view of nearby Mount Eccles.

Cordova offers many attractions, including fishing, hunting, photo trips, hiking, guided tours, flightseeing, glacier viewing, birdwatching, wildlife and scenic areas.

A typical breakfast at Cordova Rose Lodge might include sourdough pancakes, Magic Muffins, bacon or reindeer sausage, juice, coffee or tea.

JELLIED MOOSE HEAD

1 upper jawbone from a moose
1 onion, sliced
1 clove of garlic
1 T mixed pickling spices
1 t salt
1/2 t black pepper
1/4 C vinegar

Cut moose jawbone just below the eyes. Place in large kettle and boil about 45 minutes. Remove and chill in cold water. Pull out remaining hair and wash thoroughly. Place moose in kettle with fresh water. Add onions, garlic, spices and vinegar. Bring to boil and simmer until moose is tender. Let cool overnight. Take moose out of liquid and remove bone and cartilage. There are two kinds of meat, white and dark. Slice the meat thin and arrange in layers of white and dark meat in a loaf pan. Reheat the broth to boiling and pour over the moose in the loaf pan. Cool until jelly has set. Slice and serve.

EAGLE RIVER-CHUGIAK

Eagle River and neighboring Chugiak offer an abundance of restaurants, gas stations and shopping centers, plus a super-market, recreation center and library. In addition to being an active commercial hub, the area offers the following attractions: ◊Chugach State Park Visitor Center: A 13-mile drive along scenic Eagle River Road from downtown Eagle River, the center offers beautiful photo opportunities of the Chugach Mountains, hiking trails, and telescopes for wildlife viewing. Open year-round, the center also offers ranger-led hikes and naturalist programs. ◊Eagle River: Offers class II, III and IV float trips. Rangers at Chugach State Park will give information on river conditions. ◊Visitor Information Center: Located in the Valley River Mall, this center offers further information on the area.

CRANBERRY CLIFFS BED AND BREAKFAST

18735 Monastery Drive
Eagle River, Alaska 99577
(907) 696-3326 or (800) 696-7839
Tom and Maye Johnson, Hosts

Months Open: Memorial Day to Labor Day
Hours: 24
Credit Cards: MC, VISA
Accommodations: 2 rooms
Children Welcome: Yes
Pets Accommodated: No
Social Drinking: Yes
Smoking: Outside

ROOM RATES
Single w/private bath: $70
Double w/private bath: $85
Each additional person: $15
Children under 12: Free

Just a mile off the Glenn Highway, Cranberry Cliffs Bed and Breakfast is located on a hilltop which offers a lovely view of the surrounding mountains, Cook Inlet, and acres of trees. Eagle River is a mere three miles away, and it's just a 20-minute drive to downtown Anchorage.

Cranberry Cliffs guest area has a private entry, bath and convenient parking. The bedroom has a queen-size bed; the living room has a queen-size sleeper. TV, VCR and telephone are also available.

Just a short distance from Cranberry Cliffs, visitors will find bike trails, grocery stores, restaurants, six movie theaters, an Olympic-size swimming pool, skating rinks, Eklutna Native village, Thunderbird Falls and Round Top, a great mountain for climbing.

A full breakfast includes sourdough pancakes, omelettes, stuffed French toast, sweet rolls, muffins and lots of coffee. The Johnsons' sourdough starter is about 75 years old, with a unique taste that "even non-pancake eaters love."

MOM'S BERRY MUFFINS

2 C flour
1 t baking soda
1 t baking powder
3 T sugar
1/2 t salt
1 egg
1 C sour milk mixed with 2 T oil or 1 C sour cream
1 C fresh or frozen blueberries or raspberries

Mix dry ingredients. Combine egg and milk and oil or sour cream; add to dry ingredients and mix quickly (avoid over mixing). Spoon into greased or papered muffin tins and bake at 375 degrees for 20 to 25 minutes.

THE LOG HOUSE BED AND BREAKFAST

10925 Corrie Way
Eagle River, Alaska 99577
(907) 694-9231
Wayne and Joyce Simmons, Hosts

Months Open: Year-round
Hours: Until 10 pm
Credit Cards: MC, VISA
Accommodations: 2 rooms
Children Welcome: All ages
Pets Accommodated: No
Social Drinking: Yes
Smoking: Outside

ROOM RATES
Single: $60-$85
Double: $85-$100

The Log House Bed and Breakfast, 15 minutes from downtown Anchorage, is a spacious log home on a wooded lot overlooking Anchorage and the Eagle River valley.

The Log House has a large open living room with a native stone fireplace and a gift shop featuring local artists' work. The guest rooms are called the Wildflower Suite, which has a king-size bed and private bath, and the Trappers Den, which offers a queen-size bed and shared bath. Both are decorated with Alaskana and antiques. Guests can enjoy an outdoor meal at a picnic table and barbecue surrounded by beautiful flowers.

Wayne and Joyce Simmons have lived in Alaska 23 years and raised three sons. They thoroughly enjoy gardening, hunting, fishing and outdoor sports.

A full breakfast at The Log House might include pancakes, French toast, waffles, eggs, meat (ham, reindeer sausage or bacon), muffins, sweet breads or cinnamon rolls, coffee, tea, juice and milk. Fresh fruit and fresh coffee are on the table when guests wake up. Evening snacks of popcorn, fruit or ice cream are offered, and pop, juice, coffee and tea are available.

Chugach State Park and its visitor center, hiking and ski trails, as well as downhill skiing at Alpenglow, bicycle trails, river rafting and Eklutna Village Historical Park are all nearby.

LOG HOUSE OVERNIGHT CINNAMON ROLLS

4 C water
1 1/2 C sugar
1 C margarine
1 pkg yeast
4 beaten eggs
1 T salt
12 to 13 C flour

Combine water and sugar in small saucepan; boil 5 minutes. Add margarine and cool to lukewarm. Then add yeast, eggs, salt and enough flour to make a stiff dough. Knead until smooth, then place in greased bowl and let rise in warm place until double. Punch down. Let rise again. Form into cinnamon rolls — roll out in batches into a large rectangle, butter generously, sprinkle with sugar and cinnamon, roll up. Cut into slices slightly less than 1" wide. Place cut side down on heavily greased pans. Let sit on counter overnight, covered with greased wax paper. Bake in the morning at 350 degrees for 20 minutes. Glaze with powdered sugar glaze. Makes 2 dozen large rolls.

PETERS CREEK INN

22635 Davidson Road
P.O. Box 671487
Chugiak, Alaska 99567
(907) 688-2776 or (800) 680-2776; Fax: (907) 688-5031
Martha and Burl Rogers, Hosts

Months Open: Year-round
Hours: 6 am to 11 pm
Credit Cards: MC, VISA
Accommodations: 5 rooms
Children Welcome: All ages
Pets Accommodated: On approval
Social Drinking: Moderate
Smoking: Outside

ROOM RATES
Single: $65 (summer) $55 (winter)
Double: $75 (summer) $65(winter)

Peters Creek Inn is a two-story, spacious home conveniently located between Anchorage and the Matanuska Valley. The beautifully landscaped grounds overflow with colorful spring and summer flowers.

The inn offers laundry facilities, freezer space, private entrance, dining and living room facilities, TV, VCR and a barbecue and private deck for guests' use. Each of the five guest rooms has a private bath and queen or twin beds, and all have been decorated with Alaska themes: the Angler, the Prospector, the Musher, the Trapper and the Sourdough.

Peters Creek Inn serves hearty, gourmet Alaskan breakfasts, which might include eggs, sourdough pancakes, fresh-ground coffee and fresh fruit. Complimentary beverages are always available.

Nearby attractions include Eklutna Village Historical Park, Thunderbird Falls, Chugach State Park, Independence Mine State Historical Park and Knik Glacier.

RANDY'S VALLEY VIEW BED AND BREAKFAST

10131 Chandalar Street
P.O. Box 770515
Eagle River, Alaska 99577-0515
(907) 694-8266
Randy and Charles P. Polak, Hosts

Months Open: Year-round
Hours: 8 am to 9 pm
Credit Cards: None
Accommodations: 3 rooms
Children Welcome: Call for information
Pets Accommodated: On approval
Social Drinking: Yes
Smoking: No

ROOM RATES
Single: $45   Double: $55
Children up to 3 years: Free
Each additional person: $15

Randy's Valley View Bed and Breakfast is located in beautiful Eagle River Valley, a 30-minute drive from Anchorage and its International Airport. The hosts are 24-year Alaska residents, who own a mini-museum of Alaskan and European collectibles.

Randy's has a quiet, relaxing atmosphere with mountain scenery, luxurious rooms, spacious bathrooms, and a large lounge with fireplace, cable TV and VCR available. Movies on traveling in Alaska, hunting, Prudhoe Bay and other topics of interest are provided. Numerous Alaska trophies and artifacts are on display, some as old as 10,000 years. Guide and travel recommendations are available in German as well as English.

Local attractions include the famous Crow Creek Pass trail and St. Nicholas Russian Orthodox Church in Eklutna Village Historical Park, the oldest building in the Anchorage area.

Randy's Valley View Bed and Breakfast serves American and European style breakfasts on request. Special dietary needs can be accommodated with prior notice. Coffee and tea with cookies and other baked goods are also available after breakfast.

GIRDWOOD-ALYESKA

Located 37 miles south of Anchorage, Girdwood is home to Alaska's largest downhill ski area, Alyeska Resort. Alyeska offers several chair lifts, a luxury hotel and a number of restaurants. The ski lift operates year-round, for skiers in winter and sightseers in summer. An aerial tram takes visitors up to two mountainside restaurants. There is also a trail for hiking to the summit.

Other visitor attractions in the area include:

◊ Crow Creek Trail: The trail offers a short, four-mile hike to Raven Glacier. Along the trail, hikers may see gold-mining relics, Dall sheep and a beautiful alpine lake. A longer, 25-mile trail can be completed in three days, taking hikers along a portion of the historic Iditarod Trail.

◊ Portage Glacier/Begich-Boggs Visitor Center: The center overlooks Portage Glacier, Alaksa's most visited attraction, and features natural history exhibits, a 200-seat theater with daily films in summer, and an enclosed observation post.

ALYESKA BED AND BREAKFAST

P.O. Box 456
Girdwood, Alaska 99587
(907) 782-1222; Fax: (907) 782-1222
Dee Landis and Mark and Laura Lyle, Hosts

Months Open: May to September
Hours: 6 am to 9 pm
Credit Cards: All major
Accommodations: 4 Rooms
Children Welcome: Over 12
Pets Accommodated: No
Social Drinking: Yes
Smoking: On deck

ROOM RATES
Single: $95
Double: $95
Each additional person: $35

Alyeska Bed and Breakfast, nestled in Chugach State Park, is a scenic, 37-mile drive along Turnagain Arm south of Anchorage. This large cedar chalet offers an outdoor hot tub, a large deck near a small creek and a view of Mount Alyeska. The new Alyeska hotel and lodge are within walking distance.

Alyeska Bed and Breakfast sleeps six in its two-bedroom suite with living room, private bath, full kitchen, cable TV and VCR. A private studio apartment, called "Sweet Violets," provides a quiet retreat for two.

Laura, a native Floridian, came to Alaska in 1974; Mark is a native Alaskan. Dee, Laura's mother, helps with chores and loves meeting people. The Lyles also have a Yorkie named Angie.

Continental breakfast trays are available between 7 a.m. and 10 a.m. Fruit, fresh juice, muffins, sweet rolls and hot beverages are served on a tray with white linen napkins and fresh flowers.

Alyeska Bed and Breakfast is near the Portage-Whittier train depot, Portage Glacier, fishing, gold panning, hiking, bicycling, tennis, the world-famous "Bird House" bar, restaurants and gift shops. Deep sea fishing, hunting or airplane charters to land on a glacier can by arranged by reservation.

ALYESKA VIEW BED AND BREAKFAST

P.O. Box 234
Girdwood, Alaska 99587
(907) 783-2747
Heinrich and Emmy Gruber, Hosts

Months Open: Year-round
Hours: Check-in after 4 pm; check-out by noon
Credit Cards: MC, VISA
Accommodations: 3 rooms
Children Welcome: Over 6
Pets Accommodated: No
Social Drinking: Yes
Smoking: No

ROOM RATES
Room A, king-size bed: $75 double
Room B, queen and bunkbed: $75
Room C, twin beds: $70
Each additional person: $15

Hosts Heinrich and Emmy Gruber moved to Alaska from Austria in 1964 and built their own home in Girdwood. Heinrich is a carpenter, Emmy, a hairdresser. They both speak German and enjoy cross-country and downhill skiing and biking. Heinrich has trained for and run the Seward Mount Marathon race every year since 1979.

Alyeska View Bed and Breakfast is a two-story European chalet-style house surrounded during the summer by many different flowers. The upstairs deck has a view of mountains and glaciers. Alyeska Ski Resort is within walking distance, and it's just a 15-minute drive to the Portage-Whittier railroad shuttle and a 20-minute drive to Portage Glacier.

Accommodations at Alyeska View consist of three bedrooms with down comforters, a private entrance for guests and a large shared bathroom with shower and Jacuzzi.

The Grubers serve a full breakfast with omelettes, French toast, bacon and eggs or pancakes, with juice, tea, coffee and homemade breads. Snacks are served in the evenings.

Reservations are preferred, but walk-in guests are welcome. A $25 deposit will confirm reservations. Weekly rates are also available.

HALIBUT COVE

A community of commercial fishermen, artists and craftsmen, Halibut Cove qualifies as one of Alaska's most scenic settlements. Accessible only by boat or floatplane, the Cove is a mixture of large, modern homes and tiny cabins all perched on cliffs and connected by boardwalks or water. Residents take skiffs to Homer for supplies, next door to visit their neighbors or to pick up the mail.

A recently constructed art gallery in Halibut Cove features a variety of works by the Cove's artists. The Saltry, Halibut Cove's only restaurant, specializes in gourmet seafood dishes and scrumptious desserts.

Folks wishing to visit Halibut Cove for the day or overnight may take the ferry, which makes daily trips from Homer, or provide their own transportation.

QUIET PLACE LODGE
BED AND BREAKFAST

P.O. Box 6474
Halibut Cove, Alaska 99603
(907) 296-2212; Fax (907) 296-2241
Bobbie and James Jenkin and
Trina and Mike Brooks, Hosts

Months Open: Year-round
Hours: 7 am to 11 pm
Credit Cards: None
Accommodations: 5 cabins
Children Welcome: Over 15
Pets Accommodated: No
Social Drinking: Yes
Smoking: Yes

ROOM RATES
Single: $100
Double: $150 per couple
Each additional person: $75

The Quiet Place Lodge is a special getaway perched on the rocky cliffs overlooking Halibut Cove. Accessible only by boat or floatplane, a daily ferry from Homer makes getting there easy in summer. The scenery is rivaled only by the warmth of Cove residents and the abundant local wildlife.

Guests at the Quiet Place Lodge commonly arrive by ferry around 3 p.m. After a leisurely stroll around Ishmailof Island, they may choose to dine at the Saltry Restaurant, a wonderful gourmet experience, or at the lodge with advance notice.

At the lodge, guests are ensconced in private cabins furnished with antiques, books, plants and cozy comforters. A full breakfast including fruit juice, fresh melon, bacon or sausage, sourdough pancakes, eggs, wild blueberry muffins, and homemade raspberry jam is served in the lodge's dining room.

QUIET PLACE BLUEBERRY MUFFINS

2 C flour
4 t baking powder
1/2 t salt
1/2 C sugar
1 C fresh or frozen blueberries
1 egg, beaten
1/4 C shortening, melted
1 C milk

Sift dry ingredients; stir in berries. Add egg, shortening and milk; stir just until mixed. Fill greased muffin tins 2/3 full. Bake in preheated 400 degree oven for 20 to 25 minutes. Makes 18.

HATCHER PASS

Hatcher Pass and Independence Mine State Historic Park in the Talkeetna Mountains north of Anchorage are only a short drive from Palmer and Wasilla. The area is perfect for both cross-country and downhill skiing, hiking and berry picking. The alpine meadows are thick with wildflowers in summer.

Independence Mine, once a thriving gold mining operation, was shut down at the beginning of World War II. Now it is on the National Register of Historical Places. Tours of the abandoned mine buildings are offered in summer.

HATCHER PASS BED AND BREAKFAST

HC 01 Box 6797-D
Palmer, Alaska 99645
(907) 745-4210
Roxy Anderson, Hostess

Months Open: Year-round
Hours: 24
Credit Cards: MC, VISA, DC, DS
Accommodations: 3 cabins
Children Welcome: All ages
Pets Accommodated: Yes
Social Drinking: Yes
Smoking: No

ROOM RATES
Single: $55
Double: $65
Each additional person: $15
Children: $10

Hatcher Pass Bed and Breakfast is located at Mile 6.6 Fishhook Road, nine miles from Palmer and 11 miles from Wasilla. Things to see and do in the area include Independence Mine and Hatcher Pass with its fantastic views, hiking, climbing and great skiing and snowmachining in winter.

Hatcher Pass Bed and Breakfast offers clean, cozy cabins. In summer a hot tub offers a long soak after a hard day of hiking. A full breakfast — including pancakes, fresh fruit, juice, and coffee — is served in the main house or your cabin.

"At Hatcher Pass Bed and Breakfast we try our best to make you feel welcome and comfortable. We offer Alaskan log cabins ...and a full breakfast to get you on your way again. We also have a large trampoline for the kids to help release some of that energy before hitting the road to your next destination or to occupy them while you rest."

— Roxy

APPLE BLINTZES

5 eggs
3 C milk
1 1/2 t salt
1/3 C oil
3 T sugar
Flour

Whirl first five ingredients in a blender; add enough flour to make a thin batter. Grease skillet and pour in enough batter to thinly cover the bottom. Cook until lightly brown on the bottom, turn over and briefly cook other side. When done add filling and roll up like an enchilada. Serve with or without syrup.

Filling: Mix 2 pounds cottage cheese, dash of cinnamon, 2 cups shredded Monterey Jack cheese, 2 tablespoons brown sugar and 2 shredded apples in bowl.

HOMER

A highlight of any trip to Alaska, Homer is a lively town with plenty to see and lots to do. Situated 225 road miles south of Anchorage on the bluffs overlooking Kachemak Bay, Homer has a bird's-eye view of the bay and mountains and glaciers beyond.

Things to do in and around Homer include:

◊ Pratt Museum: Features collections of Native artifacts from around the bay area, aquariums of marine animals, a wide variety of marine mammal skeletons, and stuffed sea birds and animals.

◊ Homer Spit: A natural spit of land jutting out four miles into Kachemak Bay, Homer Spit is the site of the Homer Boat Harbor, deep water dock, ferry terminal, and a variety of tourist shops, restaurants, fishing charter services and commercial fishing supply stores.

◊ Art galleries: Widely known for its artists and craftsmen, Homer has several fine galleries specializing in local artwork, including pottery, watercolors, leather goods, jewelry and turned-wood bowls.

◊ Alaska Wild Berry Products: This shop makes and sells wild berry jams, jellies and candies. The store has a gift shop and window where visitors can watch the products being made.

◊ Fishing Charters: Charters abound in Homer for deep-sea halibut and salmon fishing.

◊ Halibut Cove Tour: A ferry leaves the Homer dock daily in summer for a tour of Gull Island, an immense seabird rookery, and Halibut Cove, a scenic commercial fishing village and artists' colony across the bay.

◊ Skyline Drive: Offering a panoramic view of Homer and Kachemak Bay, Skyline Drive extends from the top of East Hill Road on one side of Homer to West Hill Road on the other side.

For more information contact:

Homer Chamber of Commerce
P.O. Box 541
Homer, Alaska 99603
(907) 235-7740 or (907) 235-5300

BEACH HOUSE BED AND BREAKFAST

P.O. Box 2617
Homer, Alaska 99603
(907) 235-5945
Mary and Jack Lentfer, Hosts

Months Open: Year-round
Hours: 3 pm to 12 noon
Credit Cards: None
Accommodations: 4 rooms
Children Welcome: Over 6
Pets Accommodated: No
Social Drinking: Yes
Smoking: No

ROOM RATES
Cormorant Room:
$85 (summer) $75 (winter)
Murre and Puffin Rooms:
$60-$65 (summer) $50-$55 (winter)
Auklet Room:
$45-$50 (summer) $45-$50 (winter)
Each additional person: $25 (summer) $20 (winter)

Jack and Mary Lentfer's Beach House is — you guessed it — on the shore of Kachemak Bay in Homer. While located close to downtown, the airport and Homer Spit, the Beach House enjoys a very quiet, secluded setting with a magnificent view of the bay and the Kenai Mountains.

The house's unusual architecture results in an open and bright living space. The rooms, cheery with flowers from Mary's garden, are named after seabirds. The Cormorant Room has its own balcony, private bath with Jacuzzi, queen-size bed and bay windows. The Murre Room has twin beds and a bay window with a view of Kachemak Bay. The Puffin Room has a double bed and bay window with view; the Auklet Room has twin beds.

Hosts Jack and Mary have lived in various Alaska towns and villages, from Juneau in Southeast to Barrow on the Arctic Ocean. Before opening their bed and breakfast in Homer, Mary worked as a nurse in arctic villages and Jack worked as a wildlife biologist specializing in bears and marine mammals. Both have extensive knowledge of Alaska and Kachemak Bay.

A full, hearty breakfast — with such treats as Cardamom-Prune Drop Scones, delicate scones filled with chunks of moist prunes — is included in the price of all rooms.

"I've been very interested in bed and breakfasts the last few years and have stayed in a number of nice ones. Yours ranks right at the top for comfort, warmth and hospitality — the most important things to a steady traveler. I hope to return someday..."

— Letter from a Beach House guest

BEAR CREEK BED AND BREAKFAST

41855 Bear Creek Drive
Homer, Alaska 99603
(907) 235-8522
Carol Deitz, Hostess

Months Open: April 1 to December 1
Hours: 6 am to 11 pm
Credit Cards: None
Accommodations: 2 rooms
Children Welcome: Infants and children over 12
Pets Accommodated: No
Social Drinking: Yes
Smoking: No

ROOM RATES
Single: $45
Double: $55

Bear Creek Bed and Breakfast is located two-and-a-half miles out East End Road from the center of Homer. Going there is like going to grandma's house — over a little wooden bridge across Bear Creek. The bridge leads to a spruce-sided home surrounded by spruce and birch trees and alder and elderberry bushes. There are flowers all around and a view of Grewingk Glacier.

Inside, the house is light and airy, with rough-cut spruce beams and window trim. The lower level contains two guest bedrooms, a bathroom and a guest sitting room with books, television and VCR, a small refrigerator and a separate entrance.

For breakfast, Carol serves fresh fruit, home-baked cinnamon rolls, muffins or waffles, and juice, coffee or tea. Hot and cold cereals are available if desired.

"A walk across our bridge over Bear Creek leads guests into the peaceful atmosphere of Bear Creek Bed and Breakfast. The wooded setting with view of Grewingk Glacier, plus the comfortable bedrooms with adjoining book-filled sitting room, help make our guests' stay in the Homer area a pleasant, relaxing experience."

— Carol

FOREST LIGHT COTTAGE

P.O. Box 2613
Homer, Alaska 99603
(907) 235-2313
Phyllis Kaufman and Patrick Langdon, Hosts

Months Open: May through September
Hours: 24
Credit Cards: None
Accommodations: 1 cabin
Children Welcome: All ages
Pets Accommodated: Yes, with deposit
Social Drinking: Yes
Smoking: Outside

ROOM RATES
Single: $70
Double: $80
Each additional person: $15
Children: $5 per bed

Forest Light Cottage is a private, single-party cottage just two miles from Homer with great views of Kachemak Bay, glaciers, mountains, and frequently passing moose. Through the trees, near the hosts' house, the cottage is very private, with two stories. The large upstairs bedroom has a king- and a queen-size bed with handmade quilts, a love seat, TV and view. A full bath is also located upstairs. Downstairs is a living room and kitchen. The living room has a double hide-a-bed, coffee table, and soft chair that makes into a single bed. There is a counter with stools between the kitchen and living room. The decor is modern and homey.

Forest Light Cottage offers freezer space, a barbecue, picnic table, a deck on two sides, a full kitchen, and lots of Alaskan books and references.

Hosts Patrick Langdon and Phyllis Kaufman love to travel during the off season. Patrick is a commercial fisherman, sports fan and fix-it man. Phyllis, a former schoolteacher, is presently writing a book, consulting and leading personal growth seminars. Their two adorable Maltese dogs are very social and love to visit the cottage when invited.

Forest Light's continental breakfast includes juice, coffee, teas, assorted breads such as bagels and muffins, fresh fruit, cream cheese, jams and butter.

Homer is full of great sights and activities: birding, wildlife viewing, fishing of all kinds, glacier tours, camping, hiking, dining, art galleries, gift shops, golf, kayaking, horseback riding, photographic opportunities and much more.

HUSKY RANCH BED AND BREAKFAST

P.O. Box 1797
Homer, Alaska 99603
(907) 235-6333; Fax (907) 235-6333
Lorraine Temple, Hostess

Months Open: Year-round
Hours: 24
Credit Cards: All major
Accommodations: 1 cabin
Children Welcome: All ages
Pets Accommodated: Yes
Social Drinking: Yes
Smoking: Outside

ROOM RATES*
Summer: $60
Winter: $50
Each additional person: $10
Children: Under 12, half price
(*Rates are for 1 to 2 persons)

Husky Ranch Bed and Breakfast is run by an 11-year Alaska resident who is an avid dog musher in winter and a licensed boat captain during the summer. Located 14 scenic miles by car beyond Homer, the surrounding area is great for hiking, skiing and relaxing. The bed and breakfast is also the trailhead for Outback Kachemak Dog Sled Tours. Guests are encouraged to go for a ride during the winter and spring.

Husky Ranch provides snowshoes, sleds and cross-country skis to fit all sizes in winter. A freezer is available to store your "catch." Pet huskies will accompany you to your room on request. The cabin is large, clean and private, with full-length windows offering a spectacular view of Kachemak Bay, Kenai Mountain Range, glaciers and grazing horses. It sleeps five comfortably, has a full kitchen, stereo, TV, and collector editions of *Alaska* magazine to read.

Continental breakfasts include croissants, muffins or bagels and cream cheese, homemade jam, hot and cold cereals, fruit, yogurt, tea, coffee, juice, milk and hot chocolate. Popcorn is always available for snacking.

RECIPE FOR...A PATH TO FOREVER

20 minutes of scenic drive to "the edge of the high country"
1 charming cabin
A bounty of sled dog welcome
A ton of hospitality
Boundless views of mountains, glaciers and bay
Hours of relaxation by woodstove (after)
Hours of dog mushing, skiing, hiking, photography,
    sightseeing, fishing, clamming, boating
2 carrots to feed the horses
1/2 hour to enjoy spectacular slide show
1 bunch of incredible wildflowers (summers only)
1 2-a.m. northern lights viewing (winters only)

Mix all well according to taste. Increase any ingredient as desired; allow to fill your heart to create the perfect Alaskan memory.

KACHEMAK KIANA BED AND BREAKFAST

P.O. Box 855
Homer, Alaska 99603
(907) 235-8824
Amy Springer, Hostess

Months Open: Year-round
Hours: Check-in after 3 pm; check-out by noon
Credit Cards: None
Accommodations: 3 rooms, 1 cabin
Children Welcome: Older only
Pets Accommodated: No
Social Drinking: Yes
Smoking: No

ROOM RATES
Single: $65-$75
Double: $75-$85
Guest cabin (sleeps two): $95
Each additional person: $25
(Summer rates are given; inquire about
winter rates, in effect September 16 through April 15.)

Kachemak Kiana Bed and Breakfast, a large, comfortable home with a panoramic view of Kachemak Bay, is located about 5 miles from town on East End Road. The large living room has an open-beamed ceiling and two fireplaces to offer warmth on blustery evenings. A heated stone floor in the kitchen and den warms your feet as you pad about this warm, inviting home.

There are three guest bedrooms at Kachemak Kiana, each with a private bath, large closets and comfortable furnishings. The master bedroom has a king-size bed and a gorgeous view of the bay. The other bedrooms each have two extra-long twin beds that can be made into a king-size bed.

Completing the bed and breakfast is a small, two-story cabin located at the back of the property. It offers privacy, a queen-size bed in the upstairs bedroom, a deck off the bedroom, a full bathroom downstairs and a small sitting room for guests. The view from this little cabin is outstanding. A large, outdoor hot tub is located next to the cabin for guests' use. Robes and large towels are furnished.

Hostess Amy Springer lives downstairs in the house and is available to answer questions about Homer and Alaska. She or her daughter, Lian McMillan, can help you. Kiana is located between two of Homer's fine restaurants and there is even a small, local golf course close by. Parking is ample and an electrical hook-up for one motorhome is available. Breakfast is full continental with cereal, fruit, rolls, coffee and juice.

A "KIANA" BREAKFAST RECIPE

Start fresh and rested from a comfortable bed,
Add coffee brewing in the kitchen, no waiting to be fed,
The table is ready whenever you are,
Fresh fruit, bagels, cream cheese and jam by the jar.
Toast, juice, cereal and a muffin or two,
And just look out the window...what a view!
Mix all this easily together with proper amounts of old
Friends, new friends, sunshine and rain.
You'll appreciate it, you'll like it and
You'll want to share it again and again.

LILY PAD BED AND BREAKFAST

3954 Bartlett
Homer, Alaska 99603
(907) 235-6630
Ben and Lily Laughlin, Hosts

Months Open: Year-round
Hours: Flexible
Credit Cards: MC, VISA
Accommodations: 7 rooms
Children Welcome: Yes
Pets Accommodated: No
Social Drinking: Yes
Smoking: No

ROOM RATES
Shared bath:
$65 (summer) $45 (winter)
Private bath:
$75 (summer) $55 (winter)
(Rates are based on double occupancy.)

Lily Pad Bed and Breakfast, run by 25-year Homer residents, is centrally located within minutes of fishing, tours, the museum, arts and crafts stores, bike riding, shopping, clam digging, ferry trips, dining, kayaking, churches, and theaters.

Accommodations include a central kitchen, seven bedrooms, five baths (three of them private), and cable TV. This bed and breakfast is separate from the Laughlins' home, and is set up more like a minihotel. It was built in 1991 and has all new, firm queen-size or extra-long twin beds with nice linens. A full-service beauty and tanning salon is available on location, and the Laughlins serve a full breakfast daily.

MAGIC CANYON RANCH BED AND BREAKFAST

40015 Waterman Road
Homer, Alaska 99603
(907) 235-6077
Davis, Betsy and Taber Webb, Hosts

Months Open: Year-round
Hours: 24
Credit Cards: None
Accommodations: 4 rooms
Children Welcome: All ages
Pets Accommodated: No
Social Drinking: Yes
Smoking: Outside

ROOM RATES
Single: $55
Double: $75-$90
Each additional person: $25
Children: $20

The 75-acre Magic Canyon Ranch lies five miles out Homer's East End Road on Waterman Road, which winds uphill through meadows to the base of the secluded canyon. The road offers one the most spectacular views of Kachemak Bay in the area. Magic Canyon is the country home and llama farm of Davis, Betsy and Taber Webb. The Webbs' interests include natural history, bird-watching and quilt-making.

At breakfast, guests are served such specialties of the house as gourmet waffles with various wild berry toppings and sumptuous homemade breads.

Magic Canyon offers four guest rooms. The Glacierview, with queen-size four-poster canopy bed and handmade quilts, is a spacious suite with a magnificent view of the bay, glaciers and mountains. A perfect honeymooners' hideaway, this room has a private bath with old-fashioned tub. The brass-and-oak Northern Lights Room has granny quilts on the queen bed. This room is the "crow's nest" of the ranch house and shares a bath with the Garden Room. The sunny, south-facing Garden Room,

has twin beds and Victorian decor, with walls stenciled with fields of country roses. The Kachemak Room, set up for families or small groups with three single beds, is decorated with Homer homestead-era antiques. It has a detached three-quarter bath.

In addition to the ranch's llamas, at Magic Canyon you'll meet a plethora of songbirds, cats, dogs, and often, moose. There is a giant hot tub on the enclosed porch; Alaskana library; telescope for star-gazing; "Lizzie," a 1915 Model T; and world-class sledding in the winter.

MAGIC CANYON RAISED WAFFLES

1/2 C lukewarm water
1 pkg yeast
2 C lukewarm milk
1/2 C melted butter
1 t salt
1 t sugar
2 C flour
2 eggs
a pinch of baking soda

The night before serving, mix water and yeast in bowl; let stand 5 minutes then add milk, butter, salt and sugar. Beat in flour, cover bowl and let stand overnight (or at least 8 hours). The next morning, stir and add eggs and baking soda. Beat well. Batter should be fairly thin. Cook as usual in waffle iron.

ROOM WITH A VIEW BED AND BREAKFAST

P.O. Box 4084
332 Mountainview
Homer, Alaska 99603
(907) 235-6955
Debi Bodett, Host

Months Open: April to October
Hours: 24
Credit Cards: None
Accommodations: 2 rooms
Children Welcome: All ages
Pets Accommodated: Outside
Social Drinking: Yes
Smoking: Outside

ROOM RATES
Couple or two singles: $85
Couple and one single: $105
Two couples: $120

Room With A View is located in a private neighborhood that is centrally located within walking distance of downtown Homer. It offers the traveler spacious accommodations with a private bedroom and a queen-size bed, private bath, and a private living space with a double bed. The view of Kachemak Bay from your own private living room is spectacular.

Room With A View comes equipped to meet all of its guests' needs with a color TV, VCR, refrigerator and microwave. A continental breakfast with fresh fruit, homemade muffins and the works awaits you at your convenience.

A deluxe wood-fired sauna is also available upon request for use at the end of your day.

APPLESAUCE MUFFINS

2 C sifted pastry flour
2 t baking powder
3/4 t salt
1 t cinnamon
1/4 t allspice
1/8 t ground cloves
3/4 C brown sugar
3/4 C raisins
1/4 C unblanched almonds
4 T shortening
1 egg
1 C cold applesauce

Preheat oven to 400 degrees and grease or paper 16 large muffin cups. Sift flour, spices, and other dry ingredients together into a large bowl. Using two knives, cut shortening into dry ingredients until the mixture resembles coarse meal. Wash and pat dry (with a towel) raisins and almonds; chop the nuts. After beating the egg in a small bowl, add applesauce. Combine applesauce mixture with dry ingredients, raisins and nuts. Stir until dry ingredients are moistened but still lumpy. Do not overstir. Spoon batter into prepared muffin cups. Fill any unused cups with water to about 2/3 full. Bake in preheated oven for about 20 minutes.

THE SHOREBIRD GUEST HOUSE

P.O. Box 204
Homer, Alaska 99603
(907) 235-2107
Rose Beck and Claudia Ehli, Hostesses

Months Open: Year-round
Hours: Until 10 pm
Credit Cards: None
Accommodations: 1 efficiency guest house
Children Welcome: All ages
Pets Accommodated: No
Social Drinking: No
Smoking: No

ROOM RATES*
Two people: $110 (summer) $85 (winter)
Weekly rate: $650 (summer) $400 (winter)
Each additional person: $15 (summer) $10 (winter)
(*Prices do not include local taxes.)

The Shorebird Guest House sits on the beach of Kachemak Bay, across the bay from Grewingk Glacier. This completely self-contained guest house has its own entrance and sports a modern decor. Full kitchen, bathroom, sitting and sleeping area all flow together with a four-window view of Kachemak Bay. The guest house has bunk beds, a queen-size bed and a queen-size hide-a-bed.

Among the many amenities offered at The Shorebird are library, cable TV, woodstove, mountain bike rental, beach access, and shorebird, seabird, seal and sea otter viewing.

Claudia and Rose are both long-time Alaskans, budding naturalists and birders. They offer their clientele interesting information about birds, fauna and flora.

Breakfast is not included, but the guest house has a fully-equipped kitchen with pots, pans, appliances and dishes, and is stocked with coffees, teas and assorted meal preparation items. A baked treat welcomes guests on arrival.

Visitor activities in the Homer area include deep sea fishing, boat tours across the bay, the Pratt Museum, local artists' shops, fishing from shore, birding and beachcombing.

HUNGARIAN BUTTER HORNS

4 C flour
1/2 t salt
1 1/3 C butter
1 T dry yeast
1/4 C warm water
5 beaten egg yolks (reserve whites for meringue, below)
1/2 C sour cream
1 t vanilla
pecans or almonds, finely chopped

Combine flour and salt; cut in butter until mixture resembles coarse meal. Mix yeast and water in small bowl; add egg yolks, sour cream and vanilla; mix well. Add yeast-egg mixture to flour mixture and mix with dough hook or by hand until very well blended and all flour has been assimilated into the wet ingredients. Divide into ten balls of equal size. Flatten each ball, place on tray, cover with plastic and chill about four hours or overnight. Prepare meringue (see recipe below) and set aside. Roll out dough, one ball at a time, as you would pie crust, using powdered sugar instead of flour for rolling. Rolling must be done quickly to keep dough from getting too warm and causing the powdered sugar to melt. Roll dough as thinly as possible; spread with a thin layer of meringue. Sprinkle with finely chopped pecans or almonds. Cut into 16 to 20 pie-shaped wedges (a pizza cutter works well for this). Roll each pie-shaped wedge from wide end to the pointed end. Place on baking sheets that have been lightly sprayed with non-stick spray. Bake at 400 degrees for 12 minutes or until a light golden color. Do not overbake. Remove from sheets quickly. These pastries are time consuming to prepare, but are worth the effort. It helps to have an extra pair of hands to help. The butter horns freeze very well if stored in an airtight container.

Meringue:

Beat 5 egg whites, adding 1 1/3 C sugar 1 tablespoon at a time. Add 2 t vanilla and beat until mixture holds very stiff peaks and all sugar is dissolved.

SPRUCE ACRES
BED AND BREAKFAST CABINS

910 Sterling Highway
Homer, Alaska 99603
(907) 235-8388
John and Joyce Williams, Hosts

Months Open: Year-round
Hours: 7 am to midnight
Credit Cards: MC, VISA
Accommodations: 4 cabins
Children Welcome: All ages
Pets Accommodated: On approval
Social Drinking: No
Smoking: Outside

ROOM RATES
Guest cabins: $50-$75 (summer) $40-$60 (winter)
Each additional person: $10
Weekly rates: $10 less per night

Spruce Acres Bed and Breakfast has four cute and cozy cabins decorated in country/Victorian style. A creek and nature trail add to its "small farm atmosphere."

The cabins have private baths, color TVs, VCRs, phones, kitchenettes and living rooms. A barbecue pit may be used by guests. Alaska videos, a Nintendo game, laundry facilities, a portable crib and freezer space are available on request.

Continental breakfast including homemade breads, muffins, cinnamon rolls, juice, cereal, fresh fruit, coffee, tea or mocha, is placed in each refrigerator in the evening.

SPRUCE ACRES MOCHA

2 C powdered hot chocolate mix (such as Swiss Miss)
1 C sugar
1 C powdered creamer
1 C instant coffee powder

Stir all ingredients together, mixing well. Place 1 to 3 tablespoons in cup; add hot water. Stir and enjoy.

SUNDMARK'S BED AND BREAKFAST

(Formerly Seekins' Bed and Breakfast)
P.O. Box 375
Homer, Alaska 99603
Phone and Fax: (907) 235-5188
Teresa and Dean Sundmark, Hosts

Months Open: Year-round
Hours: 24
Credit Cards: MC, VISA
Accommodations: 4 rooms, 1 cabin, 1 apartment
Children Welcome: All ages
Pets Accommodated: Yes
Social Drinking: Yes
Smoking: Outside

ROOM RATES
Prophet's Chamber:
Single: $70   Double: $75 Each Additional Person: $10
Homestead Cabin:
Double: $95   Second Couple: $35   Fifth Person: $15
Angler's Bunk:
Single: $60   Double: $65
Alaska Room:
Single: $80   Double: $85
Glacier Room:
Single: $70   Double: $75

Sundmark's Bed and Breakfast is located two miles up East Hill Road and has an unforgettable view of Kachemak Bay and Homer Spit. It is a relaxing, comfortable place to stay year-round. In addition to all of Homer's summer activities, winter offers wildlife photography (bald eagles and moose wander through the yard) and cross-country skiing.

The Sundmarks varied accommodations suit everyone from single travelers to groups of eight. The apartment and Homestead Cabin come complete with kitchen furnishings, cable TV, microwave ovens and outdoor decks. The main house has three bedrooms with shared baths and a one-bedroom addition with a private bath and entrance. A yard, picnic table, barbecue and wood-heated sauna are also available.

Dean and Teresa serve a delicious breakfast every morning, even to early risers. The menu usually consists of pancakes, sausage, a fruit platter, hot and cold cereals, juice, coffee, tea, milk and hot chocolate.

Guests are invited to enjoy the view from the main house and browse through the Sundmarks' collection of Alaska books, maps and videos. Dean and Teresa love to share their enthusiasm for the natural beauty and adventure of Alaska.

CHEESE STRATA

12 slices buttered whole-wheat bread, crusts trimmed
1 lb Cheddar cheese, grated
6 eggs, beaten
4 C milk
1/2 T dry mustard
pepper
Ham, mushrooms, green peppers, etc. (optional)

Break bread into pieces. Add cheese and ham or other optional ingredients to bread; mix well. Put in 9" x 13" baking dish. Beat eggs; add milk, mustard, salt and pepper. Pour egg mixture over bread; refrigerate overnight. Bake 1 hour at 350 degrees. Let stand a few minutes before serving. Serves 12.

VICTORIAN HEIGHTS BED AND BREAKFAST

P.O. Box 2363
Homer, Alaska 99603-2363
(907) 235-6357
Phil and Tammy Clay, Hosts

Months Open: January to November
Hours: 8 am to 11 pm
Credit Cards: MC, VISA
Accommodations: 5 rooms
Children Welcome: Yes
Pets Accommodated: No
Social Drinking: No
Smoking: No

ROOM RATES*
Shared single: $60
Private single: $65
Shared double: $75
Private double: $85
Each additional person: $25
Children: 6 and under free
(*Rates do not include local taxes.)

This Victorian-style home is near the top of East Hill Road, with a beautiful view of Kachemak Bay and Homer Spit. The two-story home has five large bedrooms; three have private baths and two share a bath. Two of the rooms have private balconies.

Amenities at the Clays include a living room with TV, a whirlpool bath, limited freezer space, a barbecue grill, a crib and laundry facilities on request. A self-serve continental breakfast is available before 7 a.m. From 7 a.m to 9 a.m, the Clays serve a wonderful full breakfast.

"Every year, Phil and I marvel at how many wonderful people come into our lives as a result of our bed and breakfast. We love our business, and it is a pleasure to make people feel at home at Victorian Heights."

— Phil and Tammy

WANDERING STAR
BED AND BREAKFAST

265 East Pioneer Avenue
Homer, Alaska 99603
(907) 235-6788
Stan and Nikki Welles, Hosts

Months Open: Year-round
Hours: Check-in 3 pm to 6 pm; check-out by noon
Credit Cards: None
Accommodations: 3 suites
Children Welcome: Over 6 years old
Pets Accommodated: No
Social Drinking: No
Smoking: Outside only

ROOM RATES
Summer: $60-$100 per suite
Winter: From $30 per night
(Rates for weekly, monthly or extended stays
are available summer or winter.)

Wandering Star Bed and Breakfast is in downtown Homer, within easy walking distance to gift shops, the museum, library, banks and restaurants.

Wandering Star is in the style of an old country inn. An outside door leads upstairs to a second-floor area with three suites, a guest kitchen and dining area, cable TV and telephone. The suites can sleep up to eight people at one time. The building was built in 1952 as Homer's first office building.

Stan is an engineer/consultant; Nikki is a retired full-time mother who now sews and makes heirloom quilts. The Welles are members of the Professional Association of Innkeepers International. Their son Luke and his wife Laura run a pizza restaurant below Wandering Star; the restaurant is open six days a week.

A continental buffet breakfast includes coffee, tea or hot chocolate; toast or muffins; and juice. The Welles are also happy to serve milk, cold cereal, fruit and yogurt on request. The guest kitchen has a refrigerator and microwave.

WANDERING STAR MUFFINS

1 1/2 C whole-wheat pastry flour
1/4 C bran
1/3 C sugar
2 t baking powder
1/4 t salt
1 t cinnamon
1/2 t nutmeg
3/4 C whipped yam (bake 1 medium yam about 45 minutes
    at 350 degrees; let cool, then peel and whip with 1/4 to
    1/3 C water until smooth)
1 beaten egg
3/4 C milk or water
1/2 C raisins

Combine first 7 ingredients and set aside. Mix yam, egg and milk or water; add dry mixture and stir. Don't overmix. Fold in raisins and spoon into muffin tins lined with paper muffin cups. Bake at 350 degrees for 20 minutes.

(**Note:** This recipe was created by Noel Welles Maxwell, Stan and Nikki's daughter, who has a nutrition degree from Seattle Pacific University. These muffins are low in fat and taste very good.)

WILD ROSE BED AND BREAKFAST

P.O. Box 665
Homer, Alaska 99603
(907) 235-8780
Bob and Anne Haynes, Hosts

Months Open: Year-round
Hours: 24
Credit Cards: MC, VISA
Accommodations: 3 cabins
Children Welcome: All ages
Pets Accommodated: Yes
Social Drinking: Yes
Smoking: No

ROOM RATES
Summer: $85 and $125
Winter: $50 and $59
Children: Free

Wild Rose Bed and Breakfast is located in Homer, one mile up East Hill Road — look for the moose horns with flowers painted on them.

The cabins have a rustic elegance with lots of windows for enjoying the wonderful view, and new, comfortable, firm beds, private baths, and complete kitchens. They also have everything needed for a "do-your-own" breakfast: fresh muffins or apple bread ready to warm in the microwave, cereals, fresh-ground Kaladi Brothers coffee and homemade granola.

Bob and Anne came to Alaska in 1967; Bob is a long-time commercial fisherman. They have a very friendly outdoor cat and an outdoor dog who loves kids and "lives to fetch."

Guests can pick their own raspberries and strawberries in season. In summer, a gallery of eagle and other wildlife photography is offered for sale, along with an exclusive selection of one-of-a-kind Russian dolls.

WILD ROSE MICROWAVE GRANOLA

1/3 C packed brown sugar
1/4 C honey
1/4 C vegetable oil
1 t cinnamon
1 1/2 t vanilla
3 C old-fashioned oats
3/4 C almonds, coarsely chopped
1 C dried fruit or raisins

In three-quart bowl, mix sugar, honey, oil and cinnamon. Microwave on high two minutes or until boiling. Stir in vanilla— mixture will bubble. Add oats and nuts; microwave on high three minutes. Stir well. Microwave another two minutes. Stir in fruit or raisins, dump out on cookie sheet to cool and crisp. Break up and store in covered jar.

KENAI-SOLDOTNA

Twin cities 10 miles apart, Kenai and Soldotna share the attraction of being located on the Kenai River, most famous king salmon fishing river in Alaska. Home to many fishing guides and shops catering to fishing and tourism, the towns also accommodate a large number of commercial salmon fishermen who operate on the Kenai and Kasilof rivers from June through September. The two communities also offer a full range of visitor facilities, including gas stations, grocery and department stores, speciality shops, restaurants, medical facilities, etc.

Attractions in the Kenai-Soldotna area include:

◊ Fort Kenay/Kenai Historical Museum: Features Native and Russian artifacts. Operated by and located in the city of Kenai.

◊ Russian Orthodox Church/Saint Nicholas Chapel: Built in 1896, this is the oldest standing Russian Orthodox church in Alaska. The chapel, built in 1906, is the burial site of Kenai's first resident priest, Father Nicholai.

◊ Beluga Whale Lookout: Located in Kenai at the west end of Main Street, this is a good spot from which to check on weather, look for whales or watch fishing boats enter and leave the Kenai River.

◊ Kenai National Wildlife Refuge: The refuge takes in two million acres of Kenai Peninsula land. A visitors' center offers information on hiking or camping in the refuge, as well as on the resident populations of bear, moose, caribou, and wolves.

◊ Fishing charters: Just check the local Yellow Pages to find charter services offering world-class salmon fishing on the Kenai and Kasilof rivers.

For more information contact:

Kenai Chamber of Commerce
Box 497
Kenai, Alaska 99611
(907) 283-7989
or
Greater Soldotna Chamber of Commerce
Box 236
Soldotna, Alaska 99669
(907) 262-1337 or (907) 262-9814

BLAZY BED AND BREAKFAST

Box 758
Soldotna, Alaska 99669
(907) 262-4591; Fax (907) 262-4934
Mavis Blazy, Hostess

Months Open: Year-round
Hours: 24
Credit Cards: None
Accommodations: 5 rooms
Children Welcome: Yes
Pets Accommodated: Yes
Social Drinking: Yes
Smoking: Outside only

ROOM RATES
Single: $60
Double: $70
Each additional person: $10
Children: $10

Blazy Bed and Breakfast is within walking distance of the world-famous Kenai River and downtown Soldotna. The rooms are quite large and roomy, with 2,000 square feet devoted to guests, including a recreation room with a pool table, color TV, fireplace and kitchenette. The grounds are pleasant; a large deck with a barbecue is available for use and five bicycles are available for guests to tour Soldotna. Fishing and clamming are popular activities in the area.

At Blazy Bed and Breakfast, continental breakfasts include fresh fruit, toast, cereal, muffins, cinnamon rolls, juice, tea and coffee.

"Join us and experience real Alaskan living in our home. Enjoy a leisurely stroll to the best fishing in the world, or just relax on the back deck and enjoy the surroundings."

— Mavis

CAPTAIN BLIGH'S "BEAVER CREEK LODGE" AND GUIDE SERVICES

P.O. Box 4300
Soldotna, Alaska 99669
Lodge: (907) 283-7550
Home: (907) 262-7919
Clinton and Dolores (Dodie) Coligan, Hosts

Months Open: May 1 to October 1
Hours: 24
Credit Cards: None
Accommodations: 5 rooms
Children Welcome: All ages
Pets Accommodated: Yes
Social Drinking: Yes
Smoking: In lodge

ROOM RATES
Double: $90 - $125
Each additional person: Varies

Captain Bligh's is located on the banks of Kenai River, four miles upstream from Cook Inlet and three miles from downtown Kenai and the airport. It operates in secluded, private surroundings, on a private, dead-end road.

Anything a fisherperson needs, Captain Bligh's can provide — canoes, all fishing tackle, freezer space, fish smokers, coolers, tents, stoves, waders and raingear for surrounding bank fishing. Wildlife roams nearby on the property daily.

The lodge consists of two separate facilities: a Main House which houses up to eight guests; and the Lodge itself, consisting of three self-contained units, with a capacity of up to 16 people. Total capacity at Captain Bligh's is 24 guests. The Main House has one large back bedroom with adjoining bathroom, two full beds and one bunk. There is also one large upstairs room, looking out at mountains and the river and surrounded in glass, with three bunks and a bathroom. The Lodge has three units: one large, with bathroom and four bunk beds; and two smaller units, each with bathroom and two bunks.

The Coligans hire two full time employees, one female and one male, each season. They also have two guides. Capt. Bligh is a Canadian citizen who came to Alaska after the earthquake in 1964 and never returned to Canada. He is very outgoing and totally dedicated to hunting and fishing. Dodie came to Alaska in 1956. She is religious, does charity work, and is, according to her husband, "a sweetheart." A 20-pound neutered male cat lives at the Lodge and is everybody's pet.

Breakfast is continental, set out in the Main House. Lodge guests can do their own cooking or join guests in the main house. The Coligans prepare at least two full banquets a week.

THE CHALET BED AND BREAKFAST

4705 Strawberry Road
Kenai, Alaska 99611
(907) 283-4528
J.B. and Dolly Johnson, Hosts

Months Open: Year-round
Hours: 24
Credit Cards: None
Accommodations: 2 rooms, 1 cabin
Children Welcome: Over 11
Pets Accommodated: No
Social Drinking: Yes
Smoking: No

ROOM RATES
Double w/private bath: $70 (summer) $60 (winter)
Guest Cabin (sleeps 4): $125
Each Additional Person: $15

Located on Strawberry Road between Soldotna and Kenai off the Spur Highway, this bed and breakfast is a large modified chalet close to most of the area's tourist attractions, the Kenai River and Cook Inlet.

There are two spacious bedrooms at The Chalet, each with a queen-size and a double bed. The guest cottage has two large bedrooms with two double beds in each, a furnished kitchen and a full bath. Breakfast at The Chalet is full, with coffee or tea always available.

"At The Chalet Bed and Breakfast it is our desire to provide our guests the ultimate in Alaskan hospitality, to enhance the beauty and uniqueness of the Alaskan adventure."

— J.B. and Dolly

EAGLES ROOST BED AND BREAKFAST

319 Riverside Drive
Soldotna, AK 99669
(907) 262-9797; Fax (907) 262-9797
Magga and Roger Laber, Hosts

Months Open: Year-round
Hours: 4 am to 11 pm
Credit Cards: MC, VISA
Accommodations: 4 rooms
Children Welcome: Over 12
Pets Accommodated: No
Social Drinking: Yes
Smoking: Outside only

ROOM RATES
Single: $75 (summer) $50 (winter)
Double: $80 (summer) $60 (winter)
Each additional person: $20

Eagles Roost Bed and Breakfast is located on Riverside Drive in Soldotna on the bank of the Kenai River.

The home has four large, elegant bedrooms, each with two comfortable double beds with comforters and colorful bedspreads, private entrances, and gorgeous views of the river. Each deluxe bedroom at Eagles Roost has its own private bath. A lounge with cable television is available for social gatherings and relaxation. Waterfowl, squirrels, and occasionally moose and otters can be seen from the rooms. Hosts Magga and Roger offer varied breakfasts, including fruit, juices, hot and cold cereals, and egg dishes, served on china in the upstairs dining room.

Guests at Eagles Roost frequently fish from the bank of the Kenai River in back of the house, catching sockeye and silver salmon aplenty.

"Eagles' Roost Bed and Breakfast does its very best to see that guests have an enjoyable stay, feel at home and have a pleasant outdoor experience....They arrive as strangers and leave as friends."

— Magga and Roger

CREAMED EGGS

6 T butter or margarine
6 T all-purpose flour
1/2 t salt
1/4 t pepper
1/4 t paprika
1 t sweet basil
1 T parsley
3 C milk
12 hard-boiled eggs, sliced

In top part of a double boiler, melt butter or margarine, then add flour and seasonings and stir entil well blended. Add milk gradually, stirring over medium heat until smooth and thickened. Add egg slices and stir gently. Serve on toast, accompanied by sliced ham. Serves 6.

MARLOW'S ON THE KENAI

Box 2465
Soldotna, Alaska 99669
Phone and Fax: (907) 262-5218
Ken, Judy, Leanne and Neil Marlow, Hosts

Months Open: Year-round
Hours: 10 am to 11 pm
Credit Cards: MC, VISA
Accommodations: 5 rooms
Children Welcome: Yes
Pets Accommodated: No
Social Drinking: Yes
Smoking: Outside

ROOM RATES
Double: $80 (summer); $65 (winter)

Marlow's on the Kenai is a bed and breakfast located on the banks of the Kenai River, 15 minutes from Soldotna. To get there, take the Scout Lake Road or Panoramic Drive and follow the signs. This bed and breakfast is a three-story, glass-fronted home with spectacular views of the Kenai River and the Kenai Mountains from each bedroom. The guest rooms have either twin or king-size beds. Marlow's also has a large deck and riverbank picnic area available for their visitors' enjoyment.

Hosts Ken, Leanne and Neil Marlow are licensed driftboat guides and offer salmon fishing charters, birdwatching float trips, wildlife viewing, river picnics and wilderness canoe trips in addition to bed and breakfast accommodations. They also can book halibut fishing charters. They share their 6.5-acre spread with a Chesapeake Bay retriever. Guests enjoy fishing with the Marlow's guided fishing service.

Full breakfasts feature homemade bread and jellies that Judy prepares from wild berries she picks. The Marlows occasionally host barbecues and fish dinners.

"We are 25-year Alaska residents who look forward to helping our guests enjoy Alaska as much as we do. We like meeting new friends and take pleasure in getting them 'hooked on Alaska'."

— The Marlow Family

POSEY'S KENAI RIVER HIDEAWAY BED AND BREAKFAST

P.O. Box 4094
Soldotna, Alaska 99669
(907) 262-7430; Fax (907) 262-7430
Ray and June Posey, Hosts

Months Open: Year-round
Hours: 4 am to 10 pm
Credit Cards: MC, VISA
Accommodations: 10 rooms
Children Welcome: Over 11
Pets Accommodated: No
Social Drinking: Yes
Smoking: Yes

ROOM RATES
Per person: $65 (summer) $50 (winter)

June and Ray Posey's Kenai River Hideaway is a huge cedar-sided "four-plex turned bed and breakfast" on the banks of the Kenai River. It is conveniently located just 15 minutes from the Soldotna airport and 30 minutes from the Kenai airport.

The Poseys have two three-bedroom suites and two two-bedroom suites for a total of ten guest bedrooms, two of which

have private baths. June describes her rooms as "nicely furnished, contemporary" and has installed refrigerators with ice makers in each of the suites. The beautiful "honeymoon suite" comes complete with its own private bath, shower, Jacuzzi and king-size bed.

June has received "five-star ratings" from guests on the meals she serves. Breakfast at Posey's is full or continental, guests' choice. The full breakfast consists of coffee and juice, fruit, eggs, bacon, waffles or pancakes with June's own pecan maple butter. Other meals are available at an additional charge. There are barbecue grills and picnic tables in the yard for those who want to barbecue steaks or the salmon they've caught fresh just that morning.

June and Ray can arrange guided salmon fishing trips on the Kenai River, known for excellent fishing for sockeye and silver salmon, Dolly Varden and rainbow trout. Your hosts will also be glad to arrange charters and make bed and breakfast reservations out of Homer for halibut fishing.

STECKEL'S CASA NORTE

P.O. Box 2468
Soldotna, Alaska 99669
(907) 262-1257
John and Marti Steckel, Hosts

Months Open: June to September
Hours: 6 am to Midnight
Credit Cards: None
Accommodations: 2 rooms
Children Welcome: All ages
Pets Accommodated: No
Social Drinking: Yes
Smoking: Outside

ROOM RATES
Single: $45
Double: $70
Each additional person: $20

Steckel's Casa Norte is a multi-story ranch house five miles north of Soldotna in a quiet, secluded area with fantastic views of the Kenai Mountains. The Steckels are 16-year Alaska residents. John teaches and coaches at Soldotna Junior High School, and Marti is a principal at Sterling Elementary School. In addition to the bed and breakfast, they run a fishing guide business.

Casa Norte guests can expect to see an abundance of wildlife while enjoying the following amenities: a fireplace, separate kitchen area, separate family area with TV/VCR and Alaskana library, guide services, barbecue, fish storage and a large deck. There are two guest rooms, one with a king bed and one with a queen and a single, and both with private bath.

Breakfast includes juice, coffee, tea, cereals, fruits, a main dish of quiche, pancakes, waffles, pull-apart bread, eggs or French toast, a variety of breads, condiments, and occasionally a meat.

Fishing, canoeing, hiking, photography, shopping and a wildlife refuge are all nearby.

CASA NORTE PULL-APART BREAKFAST BREAD

1 pkg frozen rolls
1 pkg instant pudding (vanilla flavor is best)
1/4 C brown sugar
margarine
cinnamon

Spray a bundt pan with nonstick cooking spray. Place 3/4 bag of frozen rolls in pan, arranging them evenly. Sprinkle with 1/2 to 3/4 package instant pudding, then with brown sugar. Dot with margarine. Flavor with cinnamon. Cover and place in warm area to rise. Preheat oven to 350 degrees. Place risen bread in oven. Bake at 325 degrees for 20-25 minutes. Turn out on dish and present. Guests will love pulling them apart!

Variations: Add dried fruit, nuts, apple slices and/or nutmeg. Use maple or fruit syrup in place of brown sugar.

WOODS HOLE BED AND BREAKFAST

P.O. Box 512
Soldotna, Alaska 99669
(907) 262-9072
Holly Campbell, Hostess

Months Open: Year-round
Hours: 24
Credit Cards: None
Accommodations: 4 rooms
Children Welcome: All ages
Pets Accommodated: Yes
Social Drinking: Yes
Smoking: Outside

ROOM RATES
Single: $50 (summer) $45 (winter)
Double: $55 (summer) $50 (winter)
Children: $10

Woods Hole is located six miles south of Soldotna. The world-famous Kenai River and the Kasilof River are 10 minutes by car from the homestead. This log home, built by an Alaskan homesteader, provides a genuine Alaska experience.

The living room has a large fireplace made from local stones. A private trail leads to a lake bordering the 10-acre homestead, where a visitor can view arctic loons, ducks, moose and other wildlife. During the summer wildflowers, berries and beautiful foliage grow along the hiking trail. Other activities in the area include fishing, hiking, canoeing, cross-country skiing, horseback riding and dog sledding.

An outdoor barbecue grill is available for guests to practice their outdoor cooking. In the evening, guests can enjoy sharing tales of the day's fishing around the fire pit. Two friendly dogs will share their company.

A private entrance leads to the guest area, where there are three bedrooms and a shared bath. The first room has a queen-size waterbed; the second has a queen-size bed; and the third room has a double bed. A fourth room is available in a separate area of the house. All beds are fitted with cozy flannel sheets, and the room decor is Alaskan.

A full breakfast is served in the country kitchen. Espresso coffee and tea are always available.

Holly's special hospitality will assure you a pleasant stay at this very cozy hideaway in the woods.

WOODS HOLE BREAKFAST PIE

1 pkg refrigerated, ready-to-use pie crusts
4 eggs
1 C diced smoked ham
1 C shredded cheddar cheese
1 large diced tomato

Line a glass pie dish with one pie crust. Evenly place four eggs on crust. Place a layer of diced ham on top, then place the shredded cheese on top of the ham. Place diced tomato on top of cheese. Cover with remaining pie crust, turn edges under and seal. Cut a few small slits intop to allow steam to escape. Bake about 55 minutes at 375 degrees until golden brown. Serve hot to 6 guests.

KODIAK

Largest island in Alaska, 100-mile-long Kodiak is home of the oldest permanent European settlement in Alaska, a Russian settlement established in 1784 at Three Saints Bay. The present-day town of Kodiak, population about 6,700, is one of the largest commercial fishing ports in the United States, with hundreds of fishing boats filling the bustling harbor each year to deliver salmon, shrimp, herring, halibut and crab to local processers.

Cement bunkers mark Fort Abercrombie, one of the first secret radar installations in Alaska, and now a state park and national historical landmark. A 12-foot star halfway up the side of Old Woman Mountain is lit every year between Thanksgiving and Christmas in memory of military personnel who lost their lives in Kodiak operations.

Visitors can find much to choose from in Kodiak, including:
◊ The Baranov Museum (Erskine House): Built in 1808 as a warehouse for sea otter pelts, the museum houses exhibits of Native and Russian cultures.
◊ Russian Orthodox Church: This structure was built in 1945 to replace the original (built in 1794), which had been rebuilt twice after being destroyed by fire. The church contains paintings, icons and brasswork.
◊ Shuyak Island State Park: About 50 air miles north of Kodiak, this 11,000-acre park offers hunting, fishing and kayaking.
◊ Kodiak National Wildlife Refuge: Taking in nearly 2,500 square miles, the refuge was established to preserve the natural habitat of area wildlife, primarily the famous Kodiak grizzly. Activities enjoyed by refuge visitors include fishing, photography, backpacking, canoeing or camping.

For more information, contact:

Kodiak Area Chamber of Commerce
P.O. Box 1485
Kodiak, Alaska 99615
(907) 486-5557

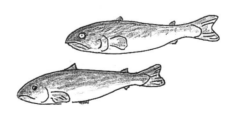

KODIAK BED AND BREAKFAST

308 Cope Street
Kodiak, Alaska 99615
(907) 486-5367
Mary Monroe, Hostess

Months Open: Year-round
Hours: 24
Credit Cards: AMEX, MC, VISA
Accommodations: 2 rooms
Children Welcome: Yes
Pets Accommodated: Yes
Social Drinking: Yes
Smoking: No

ROOM RATES*
Single w/shared bath: $60
Double w/shared bath: $72
Each additional person: $10
(*Rates do not include local taxes.)

Visitors to Kodiak Bed and Breakfast, which overlooks the downtown boat harbor, will enjoy a spectacular view of Kodiak's busy fishing fleet. Mary's contemporary home is within easy walking distance of the historic Russian Orthodox Church, art galleries, sea bird rookery, Baranov Museum and downtown restaurants and shops. This picturesque fishing city offers rich Russian heritage, stunning cliffs and beaches, abundant bird and marine life, great kayaking, hiking and biking, and, of course, fishing. Bear-viewing air charters are available. Fresh fish is often a breakfast option at Kodiak Bed and Breakfast.

WINTEL'S BED AND BREAKFAST

P.O. Box 2812
Kodiak, Alaska 99615
(907) 486-6935; Fax (907) 486-4339
Willie and Betty Heinrichs, Hosts

Months Open: Year-round
Hours: 24
Credit Cards: None
Accommodations: 4 rooms and 1 suite
Children Welcome: All ages
Pets Accommodated: No
Social Drinking: No
Smoking: No

ROOM RATES*
Single: $55
Double: $70, $80, and $90 (suite w/private bath)
Each additional person: $35
Children: $35
(*Rates do not include local taxes.)

Wintel's licensed and insured bed and breakfast is located on Mission Road, within walking distance of shops, beaches, jogging paths, hiking trails and boat harbor. The Heinrichs are 15-year residents with a wealth of information about Kodiak.

Wintel's has a Jacuzzi, Alaskana videos and books, private living room for guests and cable TV. The front window offers a beautiful view of the channel. There are five guest rooms with country decor, lots of windows and hand-quilted bedspreads. The suite has a feather bed.

Betty's cooking draws from a lifetime of collecting recipes. Breakfast is delicious: sourdough Belgian waffles and hot cakes, omelettes, freshly made sticky buns, reindeer sausage, smoked salmon, coffee cake, orange juice, coffee, herbal teas — guests' choice.

Wintel's provides a complete activity package including kayaking, road trips, hiking, flightseeing, river and ocean fishing, bear viewing, wilderness camping, and remote lodge experience. Alaska gifts are available for purchase, featuring jewelry, basketry and artwork by some of Kodiak's finest artists.

NINILCHIK

Ninilchik is a quiet little village on the Sterling Highway, about halfway between Soldotna and Homer. The community is known for excellent fishing, clamming and camping, and is supported by commercial fishing, tourism and some logging.

Things for visitors to do in Ninilchik include:

◊Russian Orthodox Church: Built in 1901, the church sits high on the bluff overlooking old Ninilchik village and Cook Inlet.

◊Deep Creek: Located two miles south of Ninilchik, the creek is an excellent spot for king salmon fishing.

◊Clam Digging: On minus tides many folks come here to dig for large, succulent razor clams.

◊Kenai Peninsula State Fair: At the end of August, Ninilchik Fairgrounds is site of the "biggest little fair in Alaska."

BLUFF HOUSE BED AND BREAKFAST

P.O. Box 39327
Ninilchik, Alaska 99639
(907) 567-3605
Terry and Margie Smith, Hosts

Months Open: Year-round
Hours: 24
Credit Cards: None
Accommodations: 6 rooms
Children Welcome: Over 16
Pets Accommodated: No
Social Drinking: Yes
Smoking: No

ROOM RATES*
Single with shared bath: $75
Double with shared bath: $85
Double with private bath: $100
(*3-day minimum; king beds available for 5-day minimum stays)

The Bluff House is centrally located on the Kenai Peninsula between the Ninilchik River and Deep Creek, a favorite vacation spot for many Alaskans. Hosts Terry and Margie Smith, long-time Alaskans, welcome guests year-round to their beautiful home with its breathtaking view of Cook Inlet. The quiet, adult atmosphere and magnificent view of three majestic volcanoes — Mount Redoubt, Mount Iliamna, and St. Augustine Volcano — make this the perfect getaway for rest and recreation.

You will find some superb freshwater fishing nearby for salmon, Dolly Varden, rainbow trout and steelhead. Cook Inlet provides some of the best saltwater fishing grounds in all Alaska and is known for its world-class king salmon and halibut, as well as excellent razor clam digging. The long days of summer bring so much to enjoy: beachcombing, wildlife viewing (guests can watch for moose, bear, fox, ermines, wolves, rabbits, a resident mountain goat that grazes on the bluff overlooking Deep Creek, and eagles soaring over tidal pools looking for dinner), picking berries and wild mushrooms, hiking, horseback riding along the beaches or trail rides up into the hills. In the winter, visitors can enjoy snowshoeing, cross-country skiing, sledding, dog sled rides and snowmachining in Caribou Hills on 150 miles of groomed, marked trails.

The Bluff House is a two-story home. The first story, dedicated to guests, has its own living room with TV/VCR, breakfast bar with refrigerator and microwave, and other

amenities to help make visits pleasant. The six guest rooms are roomy and complemented by modern facilities, including a Jacuzzi and sauna for your enjoyment after a fun-filled day.

Either a full course or continental breakfast is served according to the tides, as a majority of Bluff House guests come for the area's great fishing in the summer months.

"We do our best to make the Bluff House our guests' home away from home. You will arrive as guests and leave as friends. Our commitment is to share the beauty and uniqueness of our great state and to provide true Alaskan hospitality. We also refer our guests to fishing charters and are happy to make reservations for them."

— Margie and Terry

BLUFF HOUSE CINNAMON ROLLS

1 pkg yellow cake mix
2 pkgs dry yeast
5 C flour
2 1/2 C warm water
1 T salt
butter
brown sugar
cinnamon
nuts

Prepare topping (see below) and set aside. Combine cake mix, yeast, flour, water and salt. Put in greased bowl and let rise. Roll out; spread dough with butter and sprinkle with mixture of brown sugar, cinnamon and nuts. Roll up; cut into slices and place on topping in pans. Let rise and bake at 350 degrees until golden brown, about 35 minutes.

Topping:
1 C margarine
1 1/2 C brown sugar
1 1/2 T flour
4 T milk

Melt margarine, stir in sugar, flour and milk. Spread in bottom of two 9" x 13" pans.

PALMER-WASILLA

Palmer was established in 1935 as the destination for farmers who came to colonize the Matanuska Valley under the U.S. government's New Deal program. Today, Palmer is one of the few towns in Alaska whose residents rely on agriculture for their living. Palmer is also site of the Alaska State Fair, held the last week of August each year.

Nearby Wasilla is the restart point and headquarters of the annual Iditarod Trail Sled Dog Race to Nome. The original sled dog race has inspired many related events, celebrated together as Iditarod Days, held each March.

Activities abound for visitors to the region, including:

◊ Musk Ox Farm: Located at mile 50.1 on the Glenn Highway, this farm is home to a herd of domestic musk ox. Tours of the farm are given in the summer and you can see caretakers combing out the animals' incredibly soft wool, called *qiviut*. The wool is knitted into hats, scarves and other garments by Eskimo women.

◊ Independence Mine State Historical Park: Alaska Pacific Consolidated Mine Co. mined gold here from 1938 through 1941. Guided tours of the mine buildings are given during summer months.

◊ Matanuska Glacier: One of Alaska's most accessible glaciers, you can drive right up to this spectacular river of ice or view it from the highway.

For more information, contact:

Matanuska-Susitna Convention & Visitor's Bureau
191 E. Swanson Avenue, Suite 201
Wasilla, Alaska 99687
(907) 376-8001

ALASKAN AGATE
BED AND BREAKFAST INN

**4725 Begich Circle
Wasilla, Alaska 99654
(907) 373-2290 or (800) 770-2290
Harvey and Sandy Bowers, Hosts**

Months Open: Year-round
Hours: 9 am to 9 pm
Credit Cards: MC, VISA
Accommodations: 4 apartments
Children Welcome: All ages
Pets Accommodated: No
Social Drinking: Yes
Smoking: No

ROOM RATES*
2-bedroom apartment:
Single: $80 (daily) $69 (weekly) $30 (monthly)
Double: $90 (daily) $77 (weekly) $40 (monthly)
3 to 6 persons: $100 (daily) $86 (weekly) $50 (monthly)
3-bedroom apartment:
3 to 6 persons: $150 (daily) $129 (weekly) $60 (monthly)
(*Rates are per night, based on length of stay.)

Alaskan Agate Bed and Breakfast Inn is located midway between Palmer and Wasilla shopping and visitor attractions, just 40 minutes north of Anchorage. From the front door, it's a short drive to beautiful Matanuska and Knik glaciers, Hatcher Pass Recreation Area and Independence Mine, or spectacular Mount McKinley.

Accommodations consist of private vacation apartments, each with a full kitchen, living room and private bathroom. Laundry facilities, guest phone and freezer are also available.

A comfortable, homey atmosphere enables you to set your own schedule and enjoy a self-serve breakfast at your leisure. The kitchens are stocked with juice, coffee, tea, milk, cocoa, hot and cold cereals, eggs, waffles, toast and muffins. Guests are welcome to use the kitchens to cook other meals at their convenience.

Furnishings at the Alaskan Agate Inn are contemporary with a few antiques. Twin, full, queen-size and king-size beds are available. Guests can enjoy the collection of Alaska books, photos, maps and rock collections displayed throughout the bed and breakfast.

The hosts are 24-year Alaska residents who have traveled and worked throughout Alaska. Harvey is a geologist and energy efficiency consultant.

SMOKED SALMON SPREAD

8 oz. cream cheese, softened
1 T Worcestershire sauce
salt to taste
8 oz. sour cream
1 C smoked salmon, flaked

Mix all ingredients. May be used immediately, but will develop more flavor if prepared at least 30 minutes before serving. Serve on omelette with toast. Also great for parties and snacks throughout the day with chips or crackers.

LAKESHORE BED AND BREAKFAST

1701 W. Tillicum Avenue
Wasilla, Alaska 99654
Phone and Fax: (907) 376-1380
Yvonne and Joe Clauson, Hosts

Months Open: Year-round
Hours: 24
Credit Cards: None
Accommodations: 3 rooms
Children Welcome: Yes
Pets Accommodated: No
Social Drinking: No
Smoking: Outside

ROOM RATES*
Single: $55 (summer); $50 (winter)
Double: $65 (summer); $55 (winter)
Each additional person: $15
(*Rates given do not includelocal taxes.)

Lakeshore Bed and Breakfast offers scenic mountain vistas and a peaceful, wooded setting on the south shore of Lake Lucille in Wasilla. A large, four-bedroom home right on the water, Lakeshore provides special extras such as a paddle boat and freezer space. All rooms have private baths and TVs. The home has a large wraparound deck, and two of the bedrooms have smaller, private decks. The hosts own a husky dog team and occasionally offer dog sled rides.

A full breakfast includes fruit or juice; eggs, French toast or pancakes; meat, such as bacon or sausage; and fresh coffee.

APRICOT-NECTAR DRESSING

1 T brown sugar
1/8 t ground cinnamon
dash nutmeg
1/2 C plain, low-fat yogurt
1/4 to 1/2 C apricot nectar
　　(amount depends on how thick you want dressing)

Stir brown sugar, cinnamon and nutmeg into yogurt. Add nectar and mix until smooth. Use on fruit salad. Keeps refrgerated up to 2 weeks. Makes 1 cup.

LAKESHORE SAUSAGE SCRAMBLE

1 1/2 lb pork sausage
18 eggs
2 C milk
3 C shredded cheese
3 C garlic- and onion-flavored croutons

Cook sausage over medium heat until light brown. Drain. Place sausage in 9" x 13" baking dish. Beat eggs and milk. Stir in cheese. Pour egg mixture over sausage; sprinkle with croutons. Bake uncovered at 350 degrees until knife inserted in center comes out fairly clean, 45 to 50 minutes. (Recipe may be prepared and refrigerated the night before, but do not put croutons on until ready to bake).

Let stand 5 minutes before serving. You may serve sliced tomato, avocado, sour cream, etc. as a garnish.

SOUTHSHORE BED AND BREAKFAST

Box 870723
Wasilla, Alaska 99687
(907) 376-9334
Helen and Jim Messick, Hosts

Months Open: Year-round
Hours: 8 am to 10 pm
Credit Cards: MC, VISA
Accommodations: 1 cabin (2 adults, 1 child)
Children Welcome: Over 6
Pets Accommodated: No
Social Drinking: No
Smoking: Outside

ROOM RATES
Single: $70 (summer) $50 (winter)
Double: $85 (summer) $65 (winter)
Each additional person: $20

Southshore Bed and Breakfast is located within a few miles of a medical center, a number of restaurants, shopping centers, the post office, churches and other facilities. The home offers a quiet, secluded lake front area for relaxation and enjoyment.

Southshore is surrrounded by woods with 225 feet fronting the shore of two-mile-long Lake Lucille, home to abundant waterfowl. There is a dock for floatplane tiedown and on-site parking for cars and recreational vehicles. The hosts offer courtesy transportation from and to the Wasilla railroad depot. A car rental is nearby for those who arrive by train and wish to sightsee during their stay in Wasilla.

The cabin is completely modern and offers total privacy, with a queen-size bed, bathroom with shower, TV, VCR, kitchen, small refrigerator, microwave, toaster oven and coffee pot. A desk is supplied with stationery for your use. A private telephone will enable you to receive calls from friends and family during your stay and board games are provided.

Breakfast is in the main house or the cabin — guests' choice. There is an extensive menu from which guests can make their breakfast choice the previous evening. Breakfast includes sourdough pancakes, waffles and homemade jams and jellies.

Guests may use the deck overlooking the lake, picnic table and barbecue at the main house, canoe, paddle boat, sailboat, dock, fish smoker, freezer space, Alaska book and film library, laundry facilities, badminton, computer, fax and printer (by arrangement). A complimentary fresh fruit and snack basket is offered to all new arrivals. In winter, guests are invited to sit in the main house around a cozy wood stove and sip coffee, Russian tea, hot chocolate or cider.

Jim and Helen can also arrange flightseeing trips or stays at other bed and breakfasts in the valley, which offer guided hikes and fishing trips, highway tours and dog sled adventures.

SOUTHSHORE CHEESE SOUFFLE

9 slices white bread (crusts removed)
8 slices sharp Cheddar cheese
1 cube (1/4 lb.) margarine or butter, softened
3 C milk
4 eggs
pepper

Butter both sides of bread and stack alternately with cheese, like a tall sandwich. Cut stack into 1-inch squares and arrange in a baking dish. Beat milk, eggs and pepper; pour over bread and cheese. Refrigerate overnight. Remove 2 hours before baking. Bake at 325 degrees for 40 to 60 minutes. Serves 4.

TIMBERLINGS BED AND BREAKFAST

P.O. Box 732
Palmer, Alaska 99645
(907) 745-4445
Buz and Alma Blum, Hosts

Months Open: Year-round
Hours: Flexible
Credit Cards: None
Accommodations: 1 room
Children Welcome: By arrangement
Pets Accommodated: No
Social Drinking: Yes
Smoking: No

ROOM RATES
Single: $55
Double: $65
Three or more days: $50-$60

Timberlings Bed and Breakfast is a log cabin on 150 acres of forested hills tucked between the Talkeetna and Chugach mountains just 12 minutes from Palmer. Both hosts are artists and craftsmen: Alma is a weaver and a potter, while Buz is an award-winning bowl-turner who also teaches bowl-turning.

The Blums have a small farm with champion dairy goats, alpacas, and a friendly dog. Wild and perennial flower gardens grow on the hillside, and the farm has a fantastic view of fields and mountains across the Matanuska River. Inside the cabin are tropical plants and exotic birds.

The guest room has an antique double bed (handmade of native spruce), a color television and a VCR. There is also an extensive Alaskana library for guests to enjoy during their stay.

The kitchen has a beautiful wood cookstove that is fired up on rainy days, and the glassed-in porch provides mosquito-free lounging. Buz and Alma serve a full breakfast with croissants, homemade jams, juice and fruit, puff pancakes with wild berry sauces, "old-style" waffles and freshly ground coffee.

"We appeal to those special travelers looking for Alaska as it really can be outside of our cities. As we wave goodbye to our guests, we have the satisfaction of knowing they have rested and eaten well and are ready to enjoy the treasures of this incredible state."

— Buz and Alma

TIMBERLINGS PUFF PANCAKES

6 T butter
1 C milk
2/3 C flour
1/2 t nutmeg or cardamom
1/2 t salt
2 eggs
2 T sugar

Melt half of butter in each of 2 8" pie pans. Mix remaining ingredients in blender. Pour half of mixture into each pie pan. Bake at 400 degrees for about 25 minutes. Pancakes will puff up and edges will brown, but will be soft in the center. Serve immediately with berry sauces or a sprinkle of freshly squeezed lemon juice and a dusting of powdered sugar.

WASILLA LAKE BED AND BREAKFAST

961 North Shore Drive
Wasilla, Alaska 99687
(907) 376-5985
Vern and Ricky Gronewald, Hosts

Months Open: Year-round
Hours: Flexible
Credit Cards: None
Accommodations: 3 rooms, 1 cabin, 1 suite
Children Welcome: All ages
Pets Accommodated: No
Social Drinking: Yes
Smoking: No

ROOM RATES

Single: $50 (summer) $45 (winter)
Double: $60 (summer) $50 (winter)
Single guest cabin, private bath:
$85 (summer) $75 (winter)
Double guest cabin, private bath:
$95 (summer) $85 (winter)
Lakeside Suite, 2 bedrooms w/private bath:
$110 (summer) $85 (winter)

Wasilla Lake Bed and Breakfast is a three-story rustic house nestled in the trees on the north shore of Wasilla Lake, with a beautiful view of the lake and Chugach Mountains.

There are three homey upstairs bedrooms furnished with antiques and country charm: the "Country Room," with double bed; the "West Room" with two extra-large twin beds; and the "Garret" with a queen-size bed. There is also a large sitting room on this level, with daybed, table and chairs, refrigerator and TV. The rooms share one large bath plus the bath on the next floor down.

The lower level Lakeside Suite has two bedrooms, one with a king-size bed and one with two twins, and a shared bath. The suite has a private entrance and full kitchen, dining area, living room with TV, VCR, fireplace, and huge windows overlooking the lake. It is ideal for families or two couples traveling together.

Guests have their choice of continental or full breakfast. Complimentary pontoon boat cruises are offered on Wasilla Lake, as well as the use of a paddle boat. Wasilla Lake's hostess is an enthusiastic gardener, who grows many indoor plants, a large vegetable garden and many annual and perennial flower gardens surrounding the house. The amazing greenery and award-winning gardens will take your breath away.

Nearby, visitors can fish for salmon in local streams or rainbow trout in the lake, and can visit Hatcher Pass, the Musk Ox Farm, museums and visitor centers. There is cross-country skiing on the lake in winter.

"Your warmth and hospitality made us feel more like friends than paying guests. Everything — the food, the beautiful antiques, the fresh flowers, the magnificent surroundings, and two of the nicest people we've met — combined to make our stay unforgettable. Hopefully, we'll be back."

— A Wasilla Lake Guest

STUFFED FRENCH TOAST

8 oz ricotta cheese
1 t vanilla
1 T brown sugar
1/2 C chopped walnuts
1 loaf French or Italian bread
4 eggs
1 C milk
pinch of nutmeg

Mix the ricotta, vanilla and brown sugar until light. Add nuts. Cut bread into 8 to 10 slices 1 1/2 to 2 inches thick. Cut a pocket in side of each slice. Spoon in 1 to 2 tablespoons of ricotta/nut mixture. Mix eggs, milk and nutmeg. Carefully dip both sides of stuffed bread into egg/milk mixture so bread is moistened. If bread gets too wet, stuffing will come out. Cook on lightly greased griddle or skillet until one side is brown, about 5 minutes, turning to brown other side. Tongs help. Or, bake in long, flat pan at 400 degrees about 10 minutes on each side until golden brown. Serve with syrup or preserves. Makes 8 to 10 servings.

YUKON DON'S
BED AND BREAKFAST INN

2221 Yukon Circle
(Mail: 1830 E. Parks Highway 386)
Wasilla, Alaska 99654
(907) 376-7472; Fax (907) 376-6515
Yukon Don and Kristan Tanner, Hosts

Months Open: Year-round
Hours: 24
Credit Cards: AMEX, MC, VISA
Accommodations: 5 rooms
Children Welcome: All ages
Pets Accommodated: No
Social Drinking: Yes
Smoking: No

ROOM RATES
Single: w/private bath $75; w/shared bath $55
Double: w/private bath $85; w/shared bath $65
Suite single w/private bath: $105 single; $115 double
Mini-suite w/private bath: $85 single; $95 double
Mini-suite w/shared bath: $65 single; $75 double
Each additional person: $10
Children: Under 5 free

Yukon Don's is located at Mile 1.5 Fairview Loop Road, four miles from Wasilla on an old homestead with a spectacular, 270-degree view of the valley.

Each spacious, comfortable guest room is decorated with authentic Alaskana, with themes such as the Hunting Room, the Fishing Room and the Denali Room. All rooms have phones. There is also a sauna and exercise room, and guests can relax in the Alaska Room, a 900-square-foot great room with pool table, cable TV, gift bar, and a library of Alaska books and videos.

The Tanners offer a continental breakfast bar featuring fresh-roasted gourmet coffee and Alaska honey and jams.

"It's like seeing Alaska without leaving the house."
— Judge William Hungate, St. Louis, MO

SELDOVIA

A small, picturesque community across Kachemak Bay from Homer, Seldovia can be reached only by boat or airplane. The town has old-time Alaska charm, with houses perched on rocky cliffs and boardwalks winding along the water's edge. Primarily a fishing community, Seldovia has gradually begun building up its tourist attractions and facilities with charter services, bed and breakfast homes and gift shops that entice visitors to come experience the community's beauty. Along with great halibut and salmon fishing, Seldovia has spectacular scenery, pleasant drives, berry picking and hiking.

For more information contact:

Seldovia Chamber of Commerce
Drawer E
Seldovia, Alaska 99663

DANCING EAGLES
BED AND BREAKFAST/CABIN RENTAL

P.O. Box 264
Seldovia, Alaska 99663
(907) 234-7627
Dan, Bill, Kris and Tim Lethin, Hosts

Months Open: May 15 to September 15
Hours: 7 am to 9 pm
Credit Cards: None
Accommodations: 5 rooms and 1 cabin
Children Welcome: All ages
Pets Accommodated: No
Social Drinking: Yes
Smoking: No

ROOM RATES
Single: $45
Cabin: $125
Each additional person: $40

Dancing Eagles Bed and Breakfast is run by the Lethin brothers, who have lived in Seldovia since 1979. The bed and breakfast, a rustic, clean and comfortable place built in the 1930s, is part of old Seldovia, on the east end of Seldovia harbor.

Dancing Eagles has a hot tub, sauna, feather pillows and a great view. There are five bedrooms of varying sizes in the main building. A cabin with kitchen and bath offers one bedroom and a sleeping loft.

The Lethins serve a delicious breakfast of smoked trout quiche, fresh fruit cup, fresh-ground coffee, scones and muffins.

Hiking, bicycle or kayak rental, mountain climbing, halibut and salmon fishign charters are all available nearby.

SMOKED TROUT QUICHE

1 9" unbaked pie crust
6 oz (about) smoked trout
1 C thinly sliced onion
1 package (8 oz) cream cheese, softened
6 eggs
1 can condensed milk
1/2 t dry mustard
2 T parsley flakes
1/4 t cayenne pepper
1/4 t salt (optional)

Layer smoked trout and onion slices in pie crust. Combine remaining ingredients, mixing well, and pour over trout and onions. Bake 1 hour at 350 degrees or until knife inserted near center comes out clean (quiche should be golden brown on top).

SEWARD

Seward is the southern end of the line for the Alaska Railroad. Like many Alaska towns, Seward has gone through its share of booms and busts, from its heyday during railroad construction to the 1964 earthquake, which destroyed 90 percent of the town. It was quickly rebuilt, and today Seward is well-known as a fishing port and tourist center.

Attractions for Seward visitors include:

◊ Kenai Fjords National Park: A 669,000-acre park which takes in Harding Icefield, a remnant of the ice age which holds some of the most rugged terrain in Alaska.

◊ Exit Glacier: Only a few miles from downtown on the edge of Kenai Fjords National Park, Exit Glacier is part of Harding Icefield. Park rangers lead walks daily in summer.

◊ Fishing and boating: With Anchorage only two hours away by road or just minutes by air, Seward has become a weekend haven for fishermen and boaters, who enjoy its sparkling clear waters and abundant marine life.

◊ Seward Silver Salmon Derby: A week-long fishing contest in which the largest silver salmon brings a prize of $10,000.

◊ Hiking Trails: Primrose Trail, Lost Lake Trail, Exit Glacier Trail and Mount Marathon Trail are just a few of the many fine hiking trails in and around Seward. The U.S. Forest Service office, located on 4th Avenue, has information on trails and cabin availability.

◊ Seward Chamber of Commerce Information Cache: Housed in a historic railroad car, the Cache has walking tour maps and information.

◊ Seward Marine Center: This branch of the University of Alaska offers films, tours of the facility and displays of marine life.

◊ Mount Marathon Run: Held each year on the Fourth of July, this grueling race to the top of the mountain and back down attracts hundreds of racers and onlookers.

For more information contact:

Seward Chamber of Commerce
P.O. Box 749
Seward, Alaska 99664
(907) 224-8051

BENSON BED AND BREAKFAST

P.O. Box 3506
Seward, Alaska 99664
(907) 224-5290
Rich and Sandy Houghton, Hosts

Months Open: Year-round
Hours: 24
Credit Cards: None
Accommodations: One room
Children Welcome: All ages
Pets Accommodated: No
Social Drinking: No
Smoking: No

ROOM RATES
Single: $75 (summer) $60 (winter)
Double: $75 (summer) $60 (winter)
Each additional person: $20
Children: $10 (2-12 years), $15 (12-17 years)

Benson Bed and Breakfast, now in its sixth year of operation, is a cedar-sided home in a quiet, wooded area which offers a single guest room. The charming room sports a country decor with white eyelet curtains and a floral bedspread on a queen-size four-poster. Guests will find a basket of soaps and toiletries in their private bathroom — including emergency disposable raingear — and the bedroom contains a library of Alaskan and children's books for reading and relaxing.

The Houghtons are a family of six. Rich teaches high school; Sandy takes care of their four children and fills the home with creative touches such as quilts, sketches and baskets. The family spent eight years in the arctic.

Breakfast is served in the family dining room. A typical breakfast includes baked custard French toast casserole served with warm rhubarb sauce, fresh fruit, juice, gourmet coffee and teas.

Fishing charters, a 24-hour grocery store, biking and hiking trails, the small boat harbor, visitor's center and Exit Glacier are all nearby.

THE FARM

P.O. Box 305
Seward, Alaska 99664
(907) 224-5691
Jack Hoogland, Host

Months Open: Year-round
Hours: 24
Credit Cards: MC, VISA
Accommodations: 11 rooms
Children Welcome: Yes
Pets Accommodated: Yes
Social Drinking: Yes
Smoking: On patios and in yard

ROOM RATES
Double: $55 - $85
Each additional person: $15

The Farm is a remodeled farmhouse on 20 acres just three miles from Seward on Salmon Creek Road. Guests at The Farm enjoy private decks and patios, barbecuing and walking in the surrounding grassy field. There are four bedrooms in the house and three sleeping cottages, most with private baths. The Farm has a slow-paced, friendly atmosphere. Jack serves a continental breakfast of toast, cereal, juice, fresh fruit and beverages.

MOM CLOCK'S BED AND BREAKFAST

P.O. Box 1382
Seward, Alaska 99664
(907) 224-3195
Marianne and Tom Clock, Hosts

Months Open: Year-round
Hours: 24
Credit Cards: None
Accommodations: 5 rooms
Children Welcome: All ages
Pets Accommodated: No
Social Drinking: No
Smoking: No

ROOM RATES
Single or Double: $55 and up (summer) $45 (winter)
Each additional person: $15
Children under 12: $10 (babies free)

Mom Clock's Bed and Breakfast is a "clean as a whistle" large country-style house three miles from Seward on the bank of Salmon Creek. Guests say staying at Mom Clock's is like "going to grandma's house" because of the homey atmosphere and the outside decor, with gingerbread trim and shutters on the windows.

The four guest rooms at Mom Clock's all have homemade quilts, and share three guest baths. One of the bedrooms has handicapped access. With the river flowing by the big back yard and mountains looming in the distance, Mom Clock's is a quiet, peaceful place to stay.

Breakfasts are full or continental, consisting of blueberry, pecan or walnut pancakes, French toast, "Mom's Movers" bran muffins, juice, coffee and tea.

TALKEETNA

As the starting point for many Mount McKinley climbs, Talkeetna receives a great number of international visitors. The town is equipped to meet the needs of these climbers with hotels, bed and breakfast homes, restaurants and laundromats.

Its residents a fun-loving bunch, Talkeetna plays host to Miner's Day, held the weekend before Memorial Day, where the action-packed outhouse race is a big attraction; and the annual Moose Dropping Festival, held the second Saturday in July, with pitching competitions and other adventurous events.

For more information contact:

Talkeetna Chamber of Commerce
P.O. Box 334
Talkeetna, Alaska 99676

BAYS BED AND BREAKFAST

P.O. Box 527
Talkeetna, Alaska 99676
(907) 733-1342
Phyllis Bays, Hostess

Months Open: Year-round
Hours: Check-in after 4 pm; check-out at 11 am
Credit Cards: None
Accommodations: 3 rooms
Children Welcome: Older children
Pets Accommodated: No
Social Drinking: No
Smoking: No

ROOM RATES
Single: $60 (summer) $55 (winter)
Double: $75 (summer) $65 (winter)
Each additional person: $20 (three people per room maximum)

Bays Bed and Breakfast is two miles from Talkeetna on all paved roads, with good highway access and a large parking lot. It is a totally modern log home set among the trees and off the road for peace and quiet. There are two shared baths with tub and shower for the three spacious guest rooms, and a TV and reading room where guests can visit with each other, share their traveling experiences, and display their videos on the VCR. The bedrooms come with double, queen-size or twin beds and comfortable furnishings.

Breakfast includes delicious fruit in season, juice, cold cereal, sweet rolls, tea and coffee.

NALI VIEW BED AND BREAKFAST

HC 89 Box 8360
Talkeetna, Alaska 99676
(907) 733-2778; Fax: (907) 733-2778
LesLee and Norm Solberg, Hosts

Months Open: Year-round
Hours: 6 am to midnight
Credit Cards: MC, VISA
Accommodations: 2 rooms
Children Welcome: Depends on bookings
Pets Accommodated: On approval
Social Drinking: Yes
Smoking: Outside in designated areas

ROOM RATES
Single: $65 (summer) $60 (winter)
Double: $85 (summer) $70 (winter)
Each additional person: $25
Children: $25

Denali View Bed and Breakfast a cozy country home with a hunting and fishing motif, is located 12 miles south of Talkeetna. It overlooks a valley with a spectacular view of Denali and the Alaska and Talkeetna Ranges.

Denali View has two rooms, both with antique and iron full-size beds and TVs. Small groups can be accommodated by using the den.

Norm has been a teacher and coach for 28 years, a hunter all his life, and a fishing guide for 20 years. LesLee has extensive experience in hospitality and is a great tour guide. Bonnie, LesLee's mom, comes to Denali View in summer to "help the guests fall in love with Alaska," as she has.

The morning's fare is a full breakfast of home-cooked specialties, fresh fruit, homemade bread, coffee and juice, served between 8 a.m. and 9 a.m. unless otherwise arranged.

Denali View and the Talkeetna area have lots to offer visitors: views of 20,320-foot Denali, mountain climbing, hiking, biking, hunting, skiing, dog sledding, snow machining, lake and river fishing, birdwatching, photography, shopping in Talkeetna, or just relaxing on the deck.

TRAPPER JOHN'S BED AND BREAKFAST

P.O. Box 243
Talkeetna, Alaska 99676
(907) 733-2354
Grete Perkins and John Baker, Hosts

Months Open: Year-round
Hours: 6 am to 10 pm
Credit Cards: None
Accommodations: 1 cabin
Children Welcome: All ages
Pets Accommodated: No
Social Drinking: Yes
Smoking: No

ROOM RATES
Single: $50
Double: $60
Each additional person: $15

Trapper John's Bed and Breakfast is located on a mini-homestead near the Susitna River, yet only a short walk from the historic townsite of Talkeetna. It is adjacent to the original village airstrip — fly-in guests are welcome.

Trapper John, now retired, enjoys restoring vintage John Deere tractors. He trapped on the Kahiltna River for 17 years in the 1960s and 1970s. Grete Perkins, an avid cook and gardener, is fulfilling a dream — to live in Alaska and operate a bed and breakfast.

Trapper John's Bed and Breakfast is a historic 1920s log cabin with its original "Blazo" can roof. It is decorated with trapping memorabilia, and animal pelts hang from the ceiling. Warm plaid flannel sheets and a down comforter ensure a cozy night's rest on the double bed or double pullout futon. There is a full kitchen (tea, coffee and cocoa provided), cold running water, and the "cutest outhouse in town." The cabin, which sleeps four, is rented to only one party at a time, affording complete privacy.

Guests enjoy a full sourdough breakfast in Grete and John's new, modern cabin on the same property. Sourdough pancakes with real maple syrup, juice, fresh fruit in season, edible fresh

flowers in season, bacon or reindeer sausage, fresh-ground coffee and good conversation make up a typical Trapper John's breakfast.

The Talkeetna area is beautifully picturesque, and there's much to do: a walking tour of Talkeetna's historic district, flightseeing, mountaineering, hiking and skiing cross-country trails, salmon fishing, rafting, basking in the peace and quiet, and studying a magnificent view of the Alaska Range.

TRAPPER JOHN'S STUFFED FRENCH TOAST

1 loaf sourdough bread
2 apples, chopped
8 oz cream cheese
10 eggs (or equivalent egg substitute, such as Egg Beaters)
1 1/2 C milk
3 t cinnamon

Remove crusts and cut bread into 1" or 1 1/2" cubes. Layer half the bread cubes on bottom of a 9" x 11" pan. Layer apples, then cream cheese cubes. Top with remaining bread cubes. Mix eggs (or egg substitute), milk and cinnamon and pour over bread mixture. Bake 35 minutes at 350 degrees or until knife inserted near center comes out clean.

VALDEZ

Located on Prince William Sound, Valdez is the southern terminus for the trans-Alaska oil pipeline. Established as a gateway for Klondike gold miners, much of the town was destroyed by the 1964 earthquake. The town has been rebuilt on higher ground four miles west of its original location. Valdez has some of the nicest streets and buildings in Alaska. The town is clean, well-maintained and scenic with Prince William Sound at its foot and the Chugach Mountains behind.

Attractions in and around Valdez include:

◊ Flightseeing Tours: Several air charter services are available in Valdez to take you up for an eagle's-eye view of Prince William Sound.

◊ Boating: Charter boats are available for sightseeing or fishing on beautiful Prince William Sound.

◊ Valdez Museum: Exhibits include a model of the pipeline terminal, a 1915 parlor and a 1907 steam fire engine.

◊ Trans-Alaska Pipeline Terminal: Truly an amazing human accomplishment, the pipeline runs mostly above-ground for more than 800 miles from Prudhoe Bay, on the Arctic Ocean, to Valdez. The 48-inch-diameter pipe has a capacity of 1.16 million barrels of crude oil a day.

◊ Crooked Creek Spawning Area: Not quite a mile out on the Richardson Highway is this spawning area and fish hatchery. The bright red salmon are easily seen from the observation platform.

◊ Bridal Veil and Horsetail Falls: At Mile 13.4 and 13.8 on the Richardson Highway, these two waterfalls plunge down the sheer walls of Keystone Canyon.

For more information contact:

Valdez Convention and Visitors Bureau
P.O. Box 1603
Valdez, Alaska 99686
(907) 835-2984

GUSSIE'S LOWE STREET INN

P.O. Box 64, 354 Lowe Street
Valdez, Alaska 99686
(907) 835-4448
Bob and Joanne LaRue, Hosts

Months Open: May 1 to October 15
Hours: 24
Credit Cards: DS, MC, VISA
Accommodations: 3 rooms
Children Welcome: All ages
Pets Accommodated: No
Social Drinking: No
Smoking: No

ROOM RATES
Single: $55   Double: $60 and $80
Each additional person: $15
Children: 6-12 years: $10; 3-6 years: $5

Gussie's Lowe Street Inn is located in the "old part of the new town" of Valdez, in the original residential area built after the 1964 earthquake, within easy walking distance to downtown businesses and gift shops. They offer pickup from the ferry or bus for guests needing transportation.

Gussie's is a tastefully decorated, comfortable, ranch-style home. All three rooms have wonderful books and videos on Alaska, cable TV and VCRs, and one room has a fireplace. The mountains surrounding Valdez can be seen from each room.

Bob and Joanne have been married over 40 years and have lived in Alaska for 36 years. Both retired from the Alaska Department of Transportation, they also own the Valdez Christian Book and Coffee Shoppe.

The LaRues named their bed and breakfast after their little dog, who is now old, blind, and much photographed by guests.

On days of early ferry departures to Whittier or Seward, the LaRues serve fresh fruit, cereal, muffins, coffee and juice. Other mornings they serve pancakes, scrambled eggs and sausages, or Belgian waffles and sausages. Every day they offer fresh fruit, juice and coffee or tea. On Sundays they make bacon and cheese quiche, served with croissants and jelly.

THE BEST OF ALL BED AND BREAKFAST

P.O. Box 1578
Valdez, Alaska 99686
(907) 835-4524
Barry and Sue Kennedy, Hosts

Months Open: Year-round
Hours: 24
Credit Cards: None
Accommodations: 3 rooms
Children Welcome: Yes
Pets Accommodated: No
Social Drinking: No
Smoking: No

ROOM RATES
Single: $60 (summer) $55 (winter)
Double: $65 (summer) $60 (winter)
Each additional person: $15
Children: Under 3 free

Located in a quiet Valdez subdivision, The Best of All Bed and Breakfast is a large, cedar-sided, home where each of the guest rooms has its own personality. Guests may choose to be alone in their room with TV and VCR or to socialize in the living room, which has cathedral ceilings and is decorated in Alaskan and Asian decor. A family room with large bay window provides a beautiful view of the surrounding mountains and valleys.

In winter, Valdez offers cross-country and downhill skiing and snowmobiling.

A serve-yourself, continental breakfast is available before 7 a.m., and a special breakfast is served between 7 a.m. and 8:30 a.m. at the dining room table.

"We are looking forward to your arrival and hope that you will enjoy our beautiful all-American city. We are confident that your stay with us will be remembered for the personal touch.
— Barry and Sue

WHITTIER

Whittier was built during World War II as a port and fuel depot for military bases farther north. Access is by ferry off Prince William Sound or by train from Portage, on the Seward Highway south of Anchorage. The scenic train trip winds along Turnagain Arm and through tunnels beneath the Chugach Mountains. Once in Whittier, the marine playground of Prince William Sound is accessible for boating, fishing, or ferrying to other destinations. Whittier's attraction is in its spectacular scenery — on a clear day it is truly breathtaking — and as an entrance point to Prince William Sound.

JUNE'S WHITTIER BED AND BREAKFAST

P.O. Box 715
Whittier, Alaska 99693-0715
(907) 472-2396; Fax (907) 472-2396
June Miller, Hostess

Months Open: Year-round
Hours: 8 am to 11 pm
Credit Cards: MC, VISA (summer only)
Accommodations: 13 rooms
Children Welcome: Yes
Pets Accommodated: Depends on unit available
Social Drinking: Yes
Smoking: Designated areas

ROOM RATES
Single: $50 (summer) $45 (winter)
Double: $85 (summer) $75 (winter)
Each additional person: $15
Children under 10: Free
Groups of up to 24 people:
$35 per person (summer) $23 per person (winter)
(Full breakfast: $5 extra per person; weekly rates available)

June's Whittier Bed and Breakfast features ocean-view suites and a variety of homemade baked goods. Surrounded by the ocean, waterfalls and glaciers, this warm, comfortable bed and breakfast is located in a 14-story condominium building, built by the Army Corps of Engineers, about three blocks from the train station. A shuttle is available by request.

Hostess June also owns a fishing and charter business, and is a school teacher and personal tour guide who loves explaining "our little city." Each condo has two or three bedrooms with private tub and shower, TV and games, a variety of reading material and an array of plants.

This historical building offers a library, museum, church services, a country store and a laundromat. It has beautiful views and a warm atmosphere; coffee, tea and hot chocolate are always available in every unit.

The homestyle breakfasts include such treats as juice, toasted homemade bread, hot cereal, and muffins, or eggs, bacon, and sourdough pancakes on request. Cereal, juice, milk or muffins are available for children.

There are plenty of hiking trails, berries to pick, bicycle and sea kayak rentals, restaurants and ice cream shops. Eagles, hummingbirds, otters, sea lions, reindeer, goats, black bear, kittywakes and other wildlife can be seen in the area. Gear rental is available for stream fishing for salmon. Sightseeing and fishing charters depart daily, and the state ferry to other Alaska cities arrives and departs almost every day.

WILLOW

Located on the Parks Highway 70 miles north of Anchorage, Willow is home to about 500 people, and offers two gas stations, a grocery store and various visitor facilities, ranging from RV parks to air taxi services. Several recreational lakes are located nearby and Willow Creek provides boat launching facilities and access to the large Susitna River.

In 1976 Alaskans voted to move the state capitol from Juneau to Willow, to make government more accessible to the general public. The capitol move, an issue intensely debated among Alaskans, was later rejected by voters because of the cost involved. Most recently, in 1994, the capitol move was again put before voters, who again rejected the proposal, thereby ensuring Willow's small town status for the time being.

YOUR CABIN IN THE WOODS

P.O. Box 74
Willow, Alaska 99688
(907) 275-3688
Dave and Janice Luce, Hosts

Months Open: Year-round
Hours: 24
Credit Cards: None
Accommodations: 1 room, 1 cabin, 1 bunkhouse
Children Welcome: All ages
Pets Accommodated: Yes
Social Drinking: Yes
Smoking: No

ROOM RATES
Single: $50
Double: $58
Each additional person: $8
Children: Under 10 free

Your Cabin in the Woods is 25 miles from Deshka Landing in Willow, at Mile 10 of the Yentna River, near Mount Susitna. It can be reached by boat or snowmachine, and the Luces provide transportation for an additional fee. Fly-ins are also welcome.

Dave and Janice are long-time Alaskans with many years of wilderness experience. In summer, plants from the woods and their garden are a part of almost every meal.

During summer and fall, guests can soak in the hot tub and enjoy daytime views of mountains, and at night, the lights of Anchorage. A wide variety of birds visit; moose and black bear pass through on occasion. In winter, sleds for children and dog sled rides can be arranged.

Breakfast at Your Cabin consists of sourdough pancakes, bacon or ham, eggs, fruit juice and herbal teas or camp coffee. Because of their remote location, the Luces are happy to have guests for other meals. Cabin guests may choose instead to bring their own food and use the fully equipped kitchen.

Both the Luce home and its guest cabin were built by master log builders using the scribe-fit technique. The buildings sit atop adjacent hills, with a 360-degree view that includes Denali. Furnishings include a brass bed, down comforters and log table and chairs. One of the bedrooms opens onto a sundeck facing Denali.

Activities in the area include cross-country skiing (miles of groomed trails are separate from snowmachine trails), snowmachining, hiking, birdwatching, foraging, fishing and photography.

INTERIOR ALASKA

Interior Alaska is known for its harsh winter climate, its beautiful carpetlike tundra, and its array of wildlife, from herds of grazing caribou to small parka squirrels. Except for the area around Fairbanks, second largest city in Alaska, Interior Alaska is sparsely populated. In the Interior, you can stand on a hill and see for miles in every direction and know that relatively few people have trod here. It is wild country at its finest.

FAIRBANKS

Fairbanks, Alaska's second largest city, was first established as a trading post for area gold miners by E.T. Barnette. Once important as headquarters for companies building the trans-Alaska oil pipeline, Fairbanks today serves as supply point and transportation hub for Interior and northern communities.

Attractions for visitors to Fairbanks include:

◊ University of Alaska and University Museum: Both facilities offer special programs and tours during summer. The Georgeson Botanical Gardens offer a bright display of northern flowers. The museum features exhibits of Native culture and prehistoric Alaska.

◊ Walking Tour: Fairbanks Convention and Visitors Bureau offers a free, guided tour of the historic downtown. Brochures and maps for self-guided tours are also available at the Visitor Center.

◊ Alaskaland: The state's only "theme park," Alaskaland is set in the gold rush days and offers rides on a miniature railroad, a restored sternwheeler, museum, a salmon bake and more.

◊ Fairbanks Golden Days: A celebration of gold rush days held each July, with events including a parade, dance, raft races, outdoor concerts and pancake breakfasts.

◊ Summer Arts Festival: Two weeks of concerts and theater, visual arts and dance workshops, held from late July to early August.

◊ Gold Dredge No. 8: View this restored gold dredge at Mile 28.7 on the Steese Highway. Tours and gold panning are offered.

◊ Tanana Valley Fair: Held each August, the fair offers arts and crafts, carnival rides, food, large vegetable contests and more.

◊ Birdwatching: Thousands of geese, ducks, cranes, swans and other species migrate through Creamers Field Migratory Waterfowl Refuge each year.

For more information contact:

Fairbanks Convention and Visitors Bureau
550 First Avenue
Fairbanks, Alaska 99701
(907) 456-5774

A FIREWEED HIDEAWAY
BED AND BREAKFAST

P.O. Box 82057
Fairbanks, Alaska 99708-2057
(907) 457-2579
Ed and Dotti Keith, Hosts

Months Open: Year-round
Hours: 24
Credit Cards: MC, VISA
Accommodations: 1 room
Children Welcome: All ages (with notice)
Pets Accommodated: Outdoors
Social Drinking: No
Smoking: No

ROOM RATES
Single: $45 (summer) $35 (winter)
Double: $55 (summer) $45 (winter)
Each additional person: $10

A Fireweed Hideaway Bed and Breakfast is located in a quiet woodland less than 10 minutes from Fairbanks in the sunny hills north of town. The setting provides excellent winter aurora viewing and occasional wildlife sightings.

A Fireweed Hideaway provides a private bath, queen-size bed, homemade breads, espresso coffees, fresh fruits and mints on the pillows. There is a wood stove in the common area, TV, and a phone in the room.

The Keiths describe themselves as "a jeans-and-flannel couple, delighted to share hearth and home." They raised seven children from previous marriages, and enjoy their 18 grandchildren. Dotti, an administrative secretary at the University of Alaska, enjoys painting, flower arranging, baking and gardening. Ed, a small aircraft mechanic for 25 years in Alaska, has interesting tales of Alaskan bush pilots.

Breakfasts include fresh fruit cups, orange juice, hot homemade cinnamon rolls, gourmet coffee and choice of cereal with milk. Espresso coffees, lemonade, ice tea and homemade cookies are always available.

A hide-a-bed with innerspring mattress that can accommodate two additional people is available in the living room, which can be closed off with a folding screen.

Several fine restaurants are within 10 to 15 minutes of A Fireweed Hideaway; the area also offers hiking, pipeline viewing and Gold Dredge No. 8.

ED'S FAMOUS INDIAN CORNMEAL BREAD

1 pkg. dry yeast
1 1/2 C water, divided
1/3 C cornmeal
1/3 C molasses
1 t salt
1 T butter
3 C flour

Dissolve yeast in 1/2 C warm water; set aside. Bring the remaining cup of water to a boil; add the corn meal. Remove from heat and stir frequently until cooled, about 30 minutes. Add molasses, salt and butter. Stir in the dissolved yeast and flour. Knead approximately 10 minutes. Let rise. Knead again, and shape into loaves. Let rise until doubled. Bake in a 350-degree oven for about 1 hour or until top is golden brown.

HINT: Inserting the pan in a brown paper bag and stapling it shut keeps the top of the bread from over-baking and gives a nice golden brown to the finished loaf. This also works great for pies. If you have a bread maker, mix this according to the directions on your machine. Mix all the boiling water with the cornmeal, molasses, salt and butter, then add the rest of the ingredients to the machine after this mixture has cooled to lukewarm.

A PIONEER BED AND BREAKFAST

1119 Second Avenue
Fairbanks, Alaska 99701
(907) 452-5393 or 452-4628
Jack and Nancy Williams, Hosts

Months Open: May 15 to October 1
Hours: 24
Credit Cards: MC, VISA
Accommodations: 1 cabin
Children Welcome: All ages
Pets Accommodated: On approval
Social Drinking: Yes
Smoking: Yes

ROOM RATES
Single: $60
Double: $75
Each additional person: $10

The Williams' bed and breakfast is a renovated pioneer's log cabin, built in 1906. Its central location allows guests to easily walk downtown to shops or restaurants. Alaskaland theme park is just one mile away.

The cabin is furnished, with cable TV, telephone, tiled bath and a fully stocked kitchen. It will comfortably accommodate up to four people. Breakfast makings are provided and guests cook their own complete feast. As Jack and Nancy Williams are restaurant owners, they can direct you to the best places to eat should you choose to dine out.

AH, ROSE MARIE DOWNTOWN

302 Cowles Street
Fairbanks, Alaska 99701
(907) 456-2040
John E. Davis, Snowball the Husky, and Tyla the Cat, Hosts

Months Open: Year-round
Hours: 24
Credit Cards: None
Accommodations: 8 rooms
Children Welcome: All ages
Pets Accommodated: No
Social Drinking: Yes
Smoking: Outside

ROOM RATES*
Single: $50 and up
Double: $65 and up
(*Winter discounts and family rooms available.)

Centrally located "on the edge of downtown, three blocks from the river," Ah, Rose Marie is a refurbished 1928 home. The house has oak floors, a downstairs guest parlor and a picnic area. Guests are given full use of the house, including kitchen facilities. The house is gleaming white with bright red trim. Gorgeous flowers abound.

John serves a "light or hearty" breakfast, including fresh fruit, cereal, homemade pastries, egg dishes, and fresh-brewed coffee or tea, in the house's dining room or on the enclosed front porch. Tea and cookies are available any time, and there is a picnic table for use on warm Fairbanks days.

"At Ah, Rose Marie we offer extraordinary hospitality and truly wonderful breakfasts served on fine china with sterling silver. Guests are free to come and go at any hour."

— John

7 GABLES INN

P.O. Box 80488
Fairbanks, Alaska 99708
(907) 479-0751; Fax (907) 479-2229
Paul and Leicha Welton, Hosts

Months Open: Year-round
Hours: 7 am to 11 pm
Credit Cards: AMEX, DC, DS, MC, VISA
Accommodations: 7 rooms, 4 suites
Children Welcome: All Ages
Pets Accommodated: Yes
Social Drinking: Yes
Smoking: Restricted

ROOM RATES
Single: $90-$110 (summer) $50-$60 (winter)
Double: $90-$120 (summer) $50-$75 (winter)
Guest Suites: $75-$180 (summer) $65-$85 (winter)
Each Additional Person: $10
Children: $10

This 10,000-square-foot, Tudor-style house is located near the Chena River on 1.5 landscaped acres. The house is a short distance by car from shops, the airport and tourist attractions.

Located between the airport and the University of Alaska, 7 Gables began as a fraternity and religious hospice for students. Since becoming a bed and breakfast, the home and its hosts have received high praise from guests and official entities. In 1989, 7 Gables earned the city's Golden Heart Award for its hospitality, commitment and effort on behalf of Fairbanks visitors. 7 Gables Inn is also inspected annually by various national associations.

7 Gables offers guests a wide variety of accommodations, from single rooms to private apartments. Also offered are cable TV, phones in each room, laundry facilities, eight Jacuzzis, and canoes, boats and bikes for enjoying your stay to the fullest.

A full gourmet breakfast, served in the dining room, features crepes, quiches, sweet breads and coffeecakes.

"Our spacious home offers a retreat from the summer sun and winter chill whether it be soaking in the Jacuzzi, browsing

in the balcony library, or watching the waterfall in the stained-glass foyer from the living room."

— Paul and Leicha

7 GABLES FRITTATA

1/2 lb sausage
2 C shredded zucchini
2 green onions, chopped
1/2 t oregano
1/2 t basil
1 T packaged Italian salad dressing mix powder
6 eggs
1/2 C whipping cream
4 oz cream cheese
1 C Cheddar cheese, shredded
1 C mozarella cheese, shredded

Brown sausage, drain and place in an 8" quiche pan or pie plate. Spread the zucchini and onions over the sausage; sprinkle with seasonings. Beat eggs with cream and pour over sausage and vegetables. Cut the cream cheese into cubes and distribute evenly on top. Cover with shredded cheeses. Bake at 325 degrees for 45 minutes, or until set. Serves 6.

BEDS IN BLUE BED AND BREAKFAST

3128 Chinook Drive
Fairbanks, Alaska 99709
(907) 479-8760 or (907) 452-2598
Laverne Wood, Hostess

Months Open: May 15 to September 10
Hours: 24
Credit Cards: MC
Accommodations: 4 rooms
Children Welcome: All ages
Pets Accommodated: No
Social Drinking: On the deck
Smoking: On the deck

ROOM RATES
Single w/shared bath: $40
Double w/private bath, $50; w/shared bath, $50
Each additional person: $10
Children: $5

Beds in Blue Bed and Breakfast is a two-story duplex with three rooms downstairs — a room with queen-size bed and private bath, a twin-bed room with private bath, and a large room with both queen-size and twin beds, capable of accommodating a family of five or more. There are two living rooms for enjoying Alaska videos or television.

Downtown Fairbanks is a 10-minute drive away, and the University of Alaska is within walking distance. Guests wishing to explore Fairbanks can easily catch a bus from the University of Alaska, and both train and airport pickup is offered with advance notice.

Laverne loves the company of people from all over the world and has great stories to share. Her homemade white bread and Alaska cranberry pancakes are a hit with visitors. Beds in Blue is a very clean, no-smoking home where guests can expect great hospitality and comfort.

EASY QUICHE

16 oz sour cream
16 oz shredded cheese (Monterey Jack and Cheddar)
4 eggs (or substitute)
onions to taste (one medium)
1/2 C grated Parmesan cheese
spinach, broccoli, or ham (for filling)

Mix first four ingredients and add your choice of filling. Divide mixture between two 9" frozen pie crusts. Top with Parmesan before baking. Bake at 375 degrees 45 minutes. Makes two 9" quiches.

BELL HOUSE

909 Sixth Avenue
Fairbanks, Alaska 99701
(907) 452-3278
Kathryn LaSalle, Hostess

Months Open: Year-round
Hours: 24
Credit Cards: MC, VISA
Accommodations: 3 rooms
Children Welcome: No
Pets Accommodated: No
Social Drinking: No
Smoking: No

ROOM RATES
Single: $65 (summer) $55 (winter)
Double: $65 (summer) $65 (winter)

Bell House is traditionally appointed, offering a homelike atmosphere and styled in the fashion of Old Cape Cod. Nestled in a historical residential neighborhood and named for Kathryn's extensive collection of bells, Bell House is within easy walking distance to restaurants, shops and many visitor attractions.

Each guest room offers an exceptionally comfortable double bed. The second floor north room features a white enameled iron bed; the second upstairs room, off the small library/sitting room, boasts a mahogany four-poster. The first floor room, with direct access to the outside deck, has an antique oak bed. A candy dish filled with Hershey Kisses is placed in each room. "I give out Kisses; my guests give me hugs," says Kathryn.

Bell House serves a continental-plus breakfast consisting of fruit and melon platter, juice, muffins, toast, English muffins, assorted jams and jellies, choice of cold cereal, hot chocolate, milk, coffee and tea. Winter menu additions are hot oatmeal, French toast or waffles. You will be served in the formal dining room, in the homey kitchen or outside on the sunny deck, weather permitting.

Bell House reflects Alaskan hospitality in gracious

surroundings reminiscent of an elegant past. You are invited to play the antique pump organ and the piano. On cool or rainy days you may warm yourself by the fireplace. Balmy summer evenings under the midnight sun may be pleasantly spent on the deck, in the lawn swing or on a bench in the parklike grounds.

There are friendly cats in residence at Bell House. They are thoroughly spoiled and moderately controllable. They love people and will go out of their way to make you feel welcome, especially if you scratch them under their chins.

Kathryn, a lifelong Fairbanksan who enjoys telling stories about what life was like for a youngster growing up in Fairbanks, states: "We love Alaska and our spacious '30s vintage home. We look forward to sharing both with you!"

BIRCH GROVE INN
BED AND BREAKFAST

P.O. Box 81387
Fairbanks, Alaska 99708
(907) 479-5781 Fax (907) 479-5781
Greg and Theresa Ely, Hosts

Months Open: February to October
Hours: 24
Credit Cards: DS, MC, VISA
Accommodations: 3 rooms
Children Welcome: All ages
Pets Accommodated: No
Social Drinking: Yes
Smoking: No

ROOM RATES
Single: $50 - $70 (summer) $45 - $55 (winter)
Double: $60 - $80 (summer) $50 - $60 (winter)
Each additional person: $15
Children: $5 - $10
(Group and senior discounts are available.)

Birch Grove Inn Bed and Breakfast is in a peaceful country setting above town on three wooded acres of birch trees. It is a beautiful, three-story, custom cedar home with a cedar-and-knotty-pine interior and birch hardwood floors. There are outdoor decks for barbecueing or wildlife viewing, a reading room and living room with fireplace for guests' use. Also available: TV and video, Alaska videos, fishing equipment, goodnight mints, velour terrycloth robes in every room, gold panning equipment, and board games. The overall decor is "country eclectic," with antiques and Alaskana collectibles. There is a large yard with flower and vegetable gardens that moose like to visit.

Three large guest rooms share a full bath and a half bath. One of the rooms has a queen-size bed and a private deck overlooking a birch grove. Another has a queen-size brass bed and a single loft bed overlooking a unique garden area. The third has a double bed and a garden view. All rooms are upstairs, handsomely furnished with teak and mahogany, Alaska art, and richly colored comforters and quilts. A roll-away bed is available.

Theresa, a high school English teacher, enjoys gardening, antiques, hiking and traveling. Greg is a communications technician for Alaska Fire Service and a pilot with a Cessna 195. He enjoys scuba diving, camping, and traveling. Greg has been in Alaska for 25 years, but like Theresa, is originally from California. The Elys have a 12-year-old female yellow Lab who enjoys the guests. She is friendly and well-trained.

Breakfast at Birch Grove Inn is "hearty and healthy," and includes sourdough blueberry pancakes, cheese souffle or other house specialities; also reindeer sausage or bacon; fresh fruit salad or fruit platter; homemade muffins; cereal, yogurt, juice, coffee, tea. Breakfast is served buffet style and special diets will be accommodated. Evening snacks include crackers and cheese, sweet breads, wine or sparkling apple cider, and coffee or tea.

Birch Grove Inn is near most major attractions in Fairbanks, including the University of Alaska Museum, the Musk Ox Farm, riverboat *Discovery*, golf course, pipeline viewing area, cross-country skiing and hiking trails.

FESTIVE EGG BAKE

1 lb bulk pork sausage, cooked and drained
1/4 lb mushrooms, sliced
1/2 C sliced green onions (with tops)
2 medium tomatoes, chopped
2 C shredded Mozzarella cheese
1 1/4 C Bisquick baking mix
12 eggs
1 C milk
1 1/2 t salt
1/2 t pepper
1/2 t dried oregano leaves

Heat oven to 350 degrees. Grease a 13" x 9" x 2" baking dish. Layer sausage, mushrooms, onions, tomatoes and cheese in dish. Mix remaining ingredients; pour over sausage and vegetable mixture. Bake until golden brown and set, about 30 minutes. Serves 8 to 12.

BIRCH HAVEN INN

233 Fairhill Road
Fairbanks, Alaska 99712
(907) 457-2451
Carol Kleckner, Hostess

Months Open: Year-round
Hours: 24
Credit Cards: MC, VISA
Accommodations: 3 rooms
Children Welcome: Yes
Pets Accommodated: No
Social Drinking: Yes
Smoking: No

ROOM RATES
Single w/private bath: $70 (summer) $55 (winter)
Double w/private bath: $90 (summer) $65 (winter)
Each additional person: $15

Birch Haven Inn is a beautiful custom-built home three miles from downtown Fairbanks, close to popular cross-country skiing and hiking areas. All guest rooms at Birch Haven are quite large and are on different floors. They all have a TV and VCR, private bath with full tub and shower, and gorgeous, homemade quilts on the beds. There is one room with a jacuzzi. A computer with laser printer is available for guests' use, and homemade cookies, candy, and espresso are offered..

Your hostess is a pilot who has traveled or flown much of the state.

Area activities include hiking, boating, fishing, museums, the riverboat *Discovery*, Alaskaland, viewing the northern lights and sightseeing.

A full-course breakfast includes fresh fruit, juice, main selection and coffee, tea or hot chocolate.

EGGY EGG ROLLS

6 egg roll wrappers
1/2 lb canned or fresh-cooked asparagus
1/2 C shredded Cheddar cheese
3 eggs
1/2 C milk
2 T diced chives
salt and pepper
parsley flakes

Grease large muffin tins and press an egg roll wrapper into each cup. You can trim the edges to fit. Cut asparagus and add to the bottom of each egg roll cup. Add some cheese. Mix the eggs, milk, chives, salt and pepper and pour mixture into cups. Bake at 325 degrees for 10 to 15 minutes or until eggs are set. Sprinkle with parsley and serve with a fresh fruit cup and homemade bread.

BLUE GOOSE BED AND BREAKFAST

4466 Dartmouth
Fairbanks, Alaska 99709
(907) 479-6973 or (800) 478-6973 (in Alaska);
Fax: (907) 457-6973
Susan and Ken Risse, Hosts

Months Open: Year-round
Hours: 24
Credit Cards: AMEX, DC, DS, MC, VISA
Accommodations: 3 rooms
Children Welcome: Yes
Pets Accommodated: No
Social Drinking: Yes
Smoking: Outside

ROOM RATES*
Light Blue Room: $55
Lavender Room: $65
Dark Blue Room: $75
(*Rates do not include local tax; summer rates
are given—winter rates are $10 less.)

The Blue Goose Bed and Breakfast is located in the University West district, about five miles from Fairbanks' city center and near the airport, university, museum and riverboat *Discovery*. The city bus runs within a block of the home.

Guests at the Blue Goose enjoy a family atmosphere. Ken is a lifelong Alaskan, and Susan, from Connecticut, has lived here 20 years. The couple met while working on the trans-Alaska pipeline. They have two children, Michael (11) and Michelle (9).

The house, a tri-level frame home in a nice neighborhood, has antique furnishings and a large, fenced yard full of flowers, and a vegetable garden. Guests marvel at the beautiful broccoli, cauliflower and giant cabbages that flourish in summer.

Each of the guest rooms has a ceiling fan and TV, and all the beds have goose-down comforters. One room has a private bath and the other two rooms share a bath. The Light Blue Room has a double antique iron/brass bed; a Grandmother's Flower Garden quilt hangs on the wall. The Lavender Room has an oak double bed which belonged to Ken's grandparents, and a twin bed. A Dresden Plate quilt hangs on the wall. The Dark Blue Room has private bath, a double bed with antique brass headboard, a twin bed, and the old bentwood cradle which the Risse's children slept in, and which now holds towels. The room is decorated in Laura Ashley's Palace Garden.

The Risses live in a separate part of the home, although they do share the living room and the kitchen/dining area with the guests. A small library, VCR and piano are available to guests, as is a large closet full of board games and toys.

The full breakfasts are special at the Blue Goose. Blue Ribbon Rhubarb Pie is baked each morning and served warm. Other specialties include muffins with Alaska blueberries or lowbush cranberries. Fresh-ground coffee, fresh fruit and lots of cereals, including homemade granola, are also served. Bedtime snacks, which could be popcorn, cookies or hot fudge sundaes, are offered.

"I think the thing that makes the Blue Goose special is that we love Alaska and we...really enjoy our guests. We spend time talking and visiting with them and do everything we can to make their stay comfortable, enjoyable and memorable."

— Susan and Ken

PUMPKIN MUFFINS

1 C mashed pumpkin (fresh frozen)
1/2 C oil
1/4 C water
2 eggs
1 1/2 C flour
1/2 t salt
1 C sugar
1 t baking soda
1/4 t nutmeg
1/4 t cinnamon
1/4 t allspice
1/2 C berries
1/2 C chopped nuts
cinnamon sugar

Mix pumpkin, oil, water and eggs; set aside. Sift dry ingredients into large bowl. Combine two mixtures. Add berries and nuts. Spoon into greased muffin cups; sprinkle tops heavily with cinnamon sugar. Bake at 350 degrees for 25 minutes.

ELEANOR'S NORTHERN LIGHTS BED AND BREAKFAST

360 State Street
Fairbanks, Alaska 99701
(907) 452-2598 or (907) 479-8760
Laverne Wood, Hostess

Months Open: Year-round
Hours: 24
Credit Cards: MC
Accommodations: 4 rooms; 1 large family or group unit
Children Welcome: All ages
Pets Accommodated: No
Social Drinking: In the gazebo
Smoking: Outside only

ROOM RATES
Single w/shared bath: $50 (summer) $35 (winter)
Double w/shared bath: $55 (summer) $45 (winter)
Double w/private bath: $65
Each additional person: $10
Children: $5

Eleanor's Northern Lights Bed and Breakfast has five attractive rooms with private baths, queen-size beds and TVs. Three rooms have small refrigerators and microwaves. Candy is provided in each room. Two of the rooms have private entrances, and two can accommodate families. A fifth room has twin beds and television.

Eleanor's is a 10-minute walk to the Fairbanks visitor's center, post office, court house, train depot, library, downtown shops and restaurants. Train and airport pickup is offered with advance notice. Families are welcome.

Breakfasts include homemade bread, Alaska lowbush cranberry pancakes, cereal, coffee (made early!) and various teas. Laverne's Mexican-style scrambled egg pizza, homemade bread and cranberry pancakes are guest favorites. Laverne takes great pride in how her guests are treated and fed.

FORGET ME NOT LODGE AURORA EXPRESS

Bed & Breakfast
P.O. Box 80128
1540 Chena Ridge
Fairbanks, Alaska 99708
(907) 474-0949
Mike and Susan Wilson, Hosts

Months Open: Year-round
Hours: 24
Credit Cards: None
Accommodations: 9 rooms
Children Welcome: 4 and over
Pets Accommodated: No
Social Drinking: Yes
Smoking: In designated areas only

ROOM RATES*
Single: $65 - $125
Double: $75 - $150
(*Rates do not include local taxes.)

Forget Me Not Lodge is nestled among the towering spruce of Chena Ridge, with views of the Tanana River, Alaska Range and the city of Fairbanks. There are a variety of beautiful rooms to choose from, a huge entertainment area from which to view the northern lights, a TV room with a large collection of Alaska videos, a deck with barbecue, and a steam room for supreme relaxation. The "Lilac and Lace" suite, master of the house, spans 650 square feet with cathedral ceilings and a lovely sitting area with fabulous view. There is a relaxing private bath with tiled, six-foot Jacuzzi tub tucked under a lovely archway. The king-size bed is draped in lilacs.

Hosts Mike and Susan, two life-long Alaskans, extend a warm invitation to guests, serving a full-course breakfast family style in the main house each morning at 8 a.m. A typical breakfast menu consists of sausage, onion/mushroom/cheese omelettes, cranberry muffins, hash-brown potatoes, fresh fruit, juice and coffee.

The Wilsons are also proud to present the "Aurora Express," three authentic Alaska Railroad cars dating back to 1956, parked on the premises. These rail cars have been completely refurbished to their original splendor, and have been updated with all the modern conveniences, including private baths. Named the "National Domain," "National Emblem" and the "Golden Nellie Caboose," the Wilson's Aurora Express promises a memorable visit.

"Forget-Me-Not Lodge/Aurora Express is truly an Alaskan bed and breakfast which will leave you with fond memories you will never forget!"

— Mike and Susan

FOX CREEK BED AND BREAKFAST

2498 Elliott Highway (1.1 Mile)
Fairbanks, Alaska 99712
(907) 457-5494; Fax: (907) 457-5464
Arna and Jeff Fay, Hosts

Months Open: Year-round
Hours: 24
Credit Cards: None
Accommodations: 2 rooms
Children Welcome: Yes
Pets Accommodated: Yes
Social Drinking: Yes
Smoking: Outside

ROOM RATES
Single: $75 (summer) $49 (winter)
Double: $85 (summer) $60 (winter)
Each additional person: $15
Children: Under 5 free

Fox Creek Bed and Breakfast is 12 miles north of downtown Fairbanks in the old mining town of Fox. The superinsulated, cedar-sided house has a large deck, and its wooded location gives a quiet, secluded, rustic feeling. The aurora borealis is frequently seen between September and April, and wildlife sightings are a regular occurrence.

There are two spacious guest rooms. The upstairs room, with shared bath, can accommodate three persons comfortably. The downstairs room can accommodate four or five and has a 3/4 private bath. Each room has a futon sofa. All guests are invited to use the cozy living room with TV, VCR and wood stove. Video rentals are available nearby in Fox, and a large garage may be used for minor repairs.

Arna, who runs Fox Creek, and Jeff, a freelance videographer, enjoy skiing and snowmobiling in winter. Arna keeps many plants, several fish tanks and a terrarium with frogs, newts and toads. She also enjoys feeding a wide variety of wild birds at several feeders. Jeff is an avid motorcyclist in summer.

The town of Fox sits at the crossroads to two different hot springs, the Yukon River, the Arctic Circle and Prudhoe Bay. It also offers several excellent restaurants, gold panning, gold dredge tours, and the world famous Howling Dog Saloon.

The Fays serve a hearty Alaska-style breakfast featuring pancakes or muffins made with local blueberries, fancy French toast (the Fays' special recipe), fresh fruit, and fresh-ground coffee.

FOX CREEK FANCY FRUITY FRENCH TOAST

    1 loaf of bread
    4 eggs
    1/3 C milk
    1/2 t cinnamon
    1/2 t vanilla (optional)
    8 oz. fruit flavored cream cheese (strawberry or pineapple)

Mix eggs, milk, cinnamon and vanilla in shallow bowl. Make cream cheese sandwiches with bread and cream cheese, then dip repeatedly in egg mixture until all eggs are absorbed. Brown in a little butter or bacon fat on a medium hot griddle. Sprinkle with powdered sugar and serve with bacon, ham or sausage, warm syrup and fresh fruit. Makes 4 servings.

MARILYN'S BED AND BREAKFAST

651 Ninth Avenue
Fairbanks, Alaska 99701-4506
(907) 456-1959
Marilyn Nigro, Hostess

Months Open: Year-round
Hours: 24
Credit Cards: None
Accommodations: 3 rooms
Children Welcome: No
Pets Accommodated: No
Social Drinking: No
Smoking: No

ROOM RATES
Single: $50
Double: $65
Double & twin: $75
Queen: $75

Marilyn's Bed and Breakfast is centrally located in downtown Fairbanks, within easy walking distance of gift shops, banks, restaurants, library and post office. The bed and breakfast is two blocks from the city bus depot, five minutes from the train station and 20 minutes from the airport. Marilyn's has off-street parking, a nonsmoking policy and a miniature dauchsund.

There are three rooms available, one with a twin bed, one with a double bed and twin bed and one with an orthopedic queen-size bed. All share the bath. Reservations are recommended.

Marilyn's Bed and Breakfast promises true pioneer hospitality. Breakfast consists of homemade jams, fresh fruit, breads or muffins, coffee, tea, assorted cereals, and occasionally waffles made with 150-year-old sourdough, quiche or French toast.

MARILYN'S B & B BREAKFAST QUICHE

3 eggs
1 1/2 C milk
1/3 C margarine
1/2 t salt
1/2 C Bisquick
1 C shredded Swiss cheese
1 C chopped ham
1 t minced onion
1 C mushrooms, drained

Mix eggs, milk, margarine, salt and Bisquick in the blender; pour into greased 10" pie pan. Add remaining ingredients. Bake at 350 degrees for 40 minutes. Let stand 10 minutes before serving.

MOUNTAIN VIEW BED AND BREAKFAST

P.O. Box 80542
Fairbanks, Alaska 99708
(907) 474-9022 or (907) 388-3804 (cellular)
Chuck and Lena Callender, Hosts

Months Open: Year-round
Hours: 24
Credit Cards: None
Accommodations: 2 rooms
Children Welcome: Yes
Pets Accommodated: No
Social Drinking: Yes
Smoking: No

ROOM RATES
Single: $70 (summer) $60 (winter)
Single suite: $75 (summer) $65 (winter)
Double: $85 (summer) $65 (winter)
Double suite: $85 (summer) $75 (winter)
Each additional person: $15
Children: $15

Mountain View Bed and Breakfast sits high on a hill overlooking the Alaska Range, Mount McKinley, the city of Fairbanks, the airport and the University of Alaska. It is 10 minutes from downtown and the university, and 15 minutes from the airport. Its rural setting offers walking and bike paths, spectacular views of the northern lights, roaming moose and lots of peace and quiet. The Callenders are retired and enjoy visiting with their guests.

The home, built in 1993, has modern furniture and lots of Alaska art. There is a full kitchen with oak cabinets and island and an oak dining room suite. The master suite is located downstairs and has a large bedroom with queen-size bed, living room with queen-size hide-a-bed, TV, private bath and a private entrance with patio. The other bedroom is spacious, with a queen-size bed, lounging chairs and TV. It has a private bath and entrance.

Breakfasts include juice, fresh fruit, different types of muffins, breads, quiche, eggs, hash browns, French toast, sourdough pancakes or waffles, coffee and teas.

Fairbanks offers a wide variety of sightseeing tours and visitor attractions such as museums, gold panning, riverboat tours, Santa Claus House and tours to Denali National Park.

PEACH FRENCH TOAST

1 29-oz can sliced peaches in heavy syrup
1 C brown sugar
1/2 C butter or margarine
2 T water
5 eggs
1 1/2 C milk
1 T vanilla
1 loaf French bread (cut into 12 to 14 slices)

Drain peaches and reserve syrup. Slowly heat sugar and butter until butter melts. Add water; continue cooking until thick and foamy. Pour into 9"x13" baking dish and cool 10 minutes. Place peaches on cooled sauce and cover with slices of bread placed close together. In blender, combine eggs, milk and vanilla. Pour over bread, cover and refrigerate overnight. In the morning, remove cover and bake at 350 degrees for 40 minutes. Loosely cover with foil for last 10 to 15 minutes if browning too fast. Serve with warmed peach syrup. Serves 12 to 14.

ROSE'S FORGET-ME-NOT BED AND BREAKFAST

502 Monroe Street
Fairbanks, Alaska 99701
(907) 456-5734
Mark and Rose Ringstad, Hosts

Months Open: Year-round
Hours: 24
Credit Cards: None
Accommodations: 3 rooms
Children Welcome: Yes
Pets Accommodated: No
Social Drinking: No
Smoking: No

ROOM RATES*
w/shared Bath: $55 (summer) $40 (winter)
w/private Bath: $65 (summer) $50 (winter)
(*Rates do not include local taxes.)

Rose's Forget-Me-Not Bed and Breakfast is located within walking distance of downtown shopping centers, restaurants, banks and the post office. This bed and breakfast offers clean, pleasant and quiet surroundings in a large, two-story home.

The large living room is a good area for hosts and guests to share experiences. The circular driveway provides off-street parking. There are three guest rooms at Forget-Me-Not. Two of the rooms, one with twin beds, the other with a double, share a bath opening onto a common hall. The room with the double bed opens onto a large deck. The third room has a queen-size bed and private bath. All guest rooms are on the second floor.

A full breakfast is served, with choice of fruit, juice, French toast, omelets, pancakes, waffles, cereal, eggs and bacon.

Mark Ringstad was born in Anchorage in 1921 and moved with his family to Fairbanks in 1925. Rose came to Fairbanks in 1945 as a student at the University of Alaska. The Ringstads love Alaska and strive to make their guests' experience in the state a high point of their lives. Their credo is "Prithee may ye be happy when ye come and ecstatic when ye leave!"

STONE FROST DOWNTOWN INN

851 6th Avenue
Fairbanks, Alaska 99701
(907) 457-5337; Fax: (907) 474-0532
Randi Reed-Helton and Maggie Reed, Hosts

Months Open: Year-round
Hours: 6 am to midnight
Credit Cards: Yes
Accommodations: 5 rooms
Children Welcome: All ages
Pets Accommodated: Dogs
Social Drinking: Yes
Smoking: Outside

ROOM RATES
Suite: $85 (summer) $75 (winter)
Single: $55 (summer) $45 (winter)
Double: $65 (summer) $55 (winter)
Each additional person: $10
Children: $10

Stone Frost Downtown Inn was built in 1928 as a rooming house and, through the years, it has always been either that or a bed and breakfast. Green with dark green trim on the outside, inside the inn is filled with antique furniture, lamps and dishes. The main room has its original hardwood floor; the other rooms are carpeted. The Inn is close to shopping, Alaskaland, train and bus stations and theaters.

There are five guest rooms: one with a shared bath on the main level; three with shared bath on the second floor; and a suite. Rooms are furnished with queen-size, double and twin beds and lots of antiques. The suite boasts a sauna, steam shower, built-in bar, and microwave. There is a fireplace in the main room, with books available there and in some bedrooms, VCR on the lower level, and cable TV and phones in all rooms.

Randi Reed-Helton is a longtime Alaskan who left a career in the moving business to run Stone Frost. Her mother, Maggie, lives at the inn as resident manager. Maggie's specialties are cinnamon rolls and mothering (not necessarily in that order).

A typical breakfast at Stone Frost might include Eggs

Benedict, orange juice, fresh melon, and fresh-ground coffee or a variety of teas, served on grandmother's china. Chocolate, chips and snacks are provided in the rooms; coffee and tea are served on request and a beverage is offered on arrival.

RANDI'S EGGS BENEDICT

1/2 lb (2 sticks) butter
5 eggs
1 t Dijon mustard
1 T fresh lemon juice
pinch of cayenne
4 sourdough English muffins
8 slices Canadian bacon

Heat butter until almost boiling. Place 1 egg, mustard, lemon juice and cayenne in a blender. With blender on low speed, pour hot butter slowly into mix. Mix until it becomes a thick, lemon yellow. Turn blender off. Meanwhile, poach remaining 4 eggs, fry bacon and toast muffins. Place 2 strips of bacon and 1 egg per muffin half and pour hollandaise sauce over. Garnish with cilantro or parsley. Serves 4.

SUCH A DEAL BED AND BREAKFAST

P.O. Box 82527
Fairbanks, Alaska 99708
(907) 474-8159
Mickey and Ed Maynard, Hosts

Months Open: Year-round
Hours: 7 am to 11 pm
Credit Cards: None
Accommodations: 3 rooms
Children Welcome: 12 and over*
Pets Accommodated: No
Social Drinking: Yes
Smoking: No
(*Younger children are welcome during the off season.)

ROOM RATES
Single: $65 (summer); $55 (winter)
Double: $75 (summer); $65 (winter)

Such a Deal Bed and Breakfast is a 4,000-square-foot home located in a beautiful, quiet, three-acre setting, surrounded by birch trees and sometimes visited by moose. It is just minutes from the golf course, the University of Alaska Museum, the riverboat *Discovery* and downtown Fairbanks.

Such a Deal's three guest rooms share an extra large bathroom. The Cat Room has two twin beds; both the Flower Room and English Hunt Room have queen-size beds. A family room has a TV and VCR for guest use, and a reading room provides peace and privacy. An outside deck is the perfect spot to look for moose, listen to the birds or watch Such a Deal (Mickey's horse) and Gidget (the goat).

The Maynards enjoy a wide variety of interests and sports, including flying, skiing, golf, tennis, fishing and equestrian sports. Mickey and Ed have raised three boys in their Fairbanks home and have lived in Alaska for 25 years.

A full breakfast, served upstairs beside a large bay window, includes several selections of fresh fruit, pancakes with strawberries or peaches, French toast, coffee and juice. The continental breakfast includes fresh fruit, cereal and muffins.

The Maynards spend a lot of time visiting with their guests and making them feel at home.

"Most of our guests feel like family when they leave. Our dog and cat are very social and enjoy people."

— Mickey and Ed

HEALY

The small settlement of Healy is located off the George Parks Highway, about 10 miles from the entrance to Denali National Park. Denali Park visitors often overnight in Healy, viewing Dall sheep, caribou and the aurora borealis.

Healy has played a major role in the operation of the Alaska Railroad since 1922. The town's main industry, though, is coal mining — in fact, Healy is site of Usibelli Coal Mine, the state's only commercial coal mine. The Usibelli mine supplies coal to the University of Alaska, the military and Fairbanks area utilities, as well as for export to South Korea.

HEALY HEIGHTS FAMILY CABINS

P.O. Box 277
Healy, Alaska 99743
Phone and Fax: (907) 683-2639
Monte and Shirley Lamer, Hosts

Months Open: May through September
Hours: 8 am to 10 pm
Credit Cards: MC, VISA
Accommodations: 4 cabins
Children Welcome: Yes
Pets Accommodated: No
Social Drinking: Yes
Smoking: No

ROOM RATES*
Guest Cabins:
$100 - $120 (summer) $80 to $100 (winter)
The Chalet:
$90 (summer) $70 (winter)
Each additional person: $10
(*Rates are based on double occupancy; no single rates.
Rates do not include local taxes.)

Healy Heights Bed and Breakfast is located at Mile 247 of the Parks Highway, 12 miles north of the entrance to Denali National Park and very close to the community of Healy. Far from rustic, Healy Heights provides all the comforts of home.

Thoreau would have loved this spot, situated on 12 private wooded acres on a spruce- and aspen-covered ridge, overlooking taiga and tundra valleys north of the Alaska Range. Healy Heights is surrounded by gravel roads to hike or run, and enjoys spectacular sunsets—a peaceful setting for the entire family.

Healy Heights offers accommodations in four secluded, tastefully furnished, cedar-sided cabins, two of which have kitchens. All have heat, electricity, hot and cold running water, private baths, refrigerators, microwave ovens and outside decks, and each has its own special atmosphere. To maintain the tranquility, there are no phones or TVs in the cabins. The Chalet is a two-story cottage with two guest bedrooms sharing a full bath. It has a double sofa bed in the living room, a full kitchen and dining area. The Guest House cottage has a sleeping loft with brass double bed and a double sleeper sofa in the living room area. Aspen View cabin, built in June 1994, and the North Ridge each have one double and one single Alaskan-crafted spruce pole platform bed and will sleep three persons.

Healy Heights offers overnight cabin rental only — no food is provided, but all accommodations have their own cooking facilities. The Hosts recommend a two-night minimum stay to allow time to fully enjoy the area.

TOK

Tok, at the junction of the Alaska and Glenn highways, began as a camp for workers building the Alaska Highway during World War II. Today, in addition to providing services for those just passing through, Tok offers dog sled demonstrations, salmon bakes, many fine Native handicrafts, and campgrounds and RV parks.

For more information contact:

Tok Information Center
P.O. Box 359
Tok, Alaska 99780
(907) 883-5667

THE STAGE STOP BED AND BREAKFAST

(for Horses and People)
Box 69
Tok, Alaska 99780
(907) 883-5338 or (800) 478-5369 (in Alaska)
Mary Dale Underwood, Hostess

Months Open: Year-round
Hours: 24
Credit Cards: None
Accommodations: 3 rooms, 1 cabin
Children Welcome: All ages
Pets Accommodated: Yes
Social Drinking: Yes
Smoking: No

ROOM RATES
Single: $35-$65 (summer) $40-$55 (winter)
Double: $45-$85 (summer) $40-$65 (winter)
Guest Cabin: $45 (summer) $40 (winter)
Each additional person: $12.50
Children Under 6: Free
Horses: $15 for stall $10 for Pole Corral

The Stage Stop, a bed and breakfast for horses and people, is located on the Tok Cutoff road just 1.7 miles from downtown Tok. While this bed and breakfast accommodates horses and their riders, it is also a wonderful stop for people traveling without four-legged animals.

The Stage Stop is a comfortable log home which offers three guest rooms inside and a 10- by 16-foot "trapper cabin" nearby. The master bedroom has a queen-size bed and a twin bed, and the sewing room has a queen-size bed. The trapper cabin holds a queen-size bed and a single cot.

The inn added a new room during winter 1991 called the Equestrian Suite. It has a nice bay window, a king-size bed and two twin beds and a private bath with a two-person Jacuzzi and shower.

Mary Underwood serves a large country breakfast of fresh eggs, hash browns, toast, bacon or ham, juice, fruit and freshly ground, steaming hot coffee before 9 a.m. A continental

breakfast is available later in the morning.

Mary has a new log barn with two stalls available for the horses. Outside she has three pole pens, each of which can accommodate several horses.

"The Stage Stop is a quiet place with lots of flowers in bloom and a hammock to relax in...a homey log house with good hospitality, good beds and good food...we have room for a family with horses or a honeymoon couple."

— Mary

FRESH RHUBARB-APRICOT JAM

    2 C rhubarb, cut into small pieces
    3/4 C sugar
    1 1/2 C fresh or canned apricots*, cut into small pieces

Cook rhubarb with sugar until almost soft, then add apricots. Cook to desired doneness, stirring often to prevent sugar from burning. This jam will keep in the refrigerator for about one week.

*Peaches may be substituted.

INDEXES

BED AND BREAKFAST HOMES

RECIPES

LISTING REQUEST FORM

If you would like to have your Bed and Breakfast included in future editions of *Bed and Breakfast Alaska Style!*, please send us your name and address and we will send you a questionnaire the next time the book is updated. (There is a fee for listing.)

YOUR NAME _____

B&B NAME _____

ADDRESS _____

CITY/STATE/ZIP _____

MAIL THIS FORM TO:

BED & BREAKFAST ALASKA STYLE!
P.O. Box 470
Homer, AK 99603

— — — — — — — — — – CLIP HERE – — — — — — — — — —

LISTING REQUEST FORM

If you would like to have your Bed and Breakfast included in future editions of *Bed and Breakfast Alaska Style!*, please send us your name and address and we will send you a questionnaire the next time the book is updated. (There is a fee for listing.)

YOUR NAME _____

B&B NAME _____

ADDRESS _____

CITY/STATE/ZIP _____

MAIL THIS FORM TO:

BED & BREAKFAST ALASKA STYLE!
P.O. Box 470
Homer, AK 99603

ORDER FORM

Please send me ___ copies of *Bed and Breakfast Alaska Style!*
For each copy I am enclosing $16.95 plus postage and handling
of $3 for first book ordered, $.50 for each additional book.

TOTAL NUMBER OF BOOKS ORDERED _____

TOTAL AMOUNT ENCLOSED $_____

YOUR NAME _____

ADDRESS _____

CITY/STATE/ZIP _____

MAIL THIS FORM WITH PAYMENT TO:

BED & BREAKFAST ALASKA STYLE!
P.O. Box 470
Homer, AK 99603

— — — — — — — — — - CLIP HERE - — — — — — — — — —

ORDER FORM

Please send me ___ copies of *Bed and Breakfast Alaska Style!*
For each copy I am enclosing $16.95 plus postage and handling
of $3 for first book ordered, $.50 for each additional book.

TOTAL NUMBER OF BOOKS ORDERED _____

TOTAL AMOUNT ENCLOSED $_____

YOUR NAME _____

ADDRESS _____

CITY/STATE/ZIP _____

MAIL THIS FORM WITH PAYMENT TO:

BED & BREAKFAST ALASKA STYLE!
P.O. Box 470
Homer, AK 99603